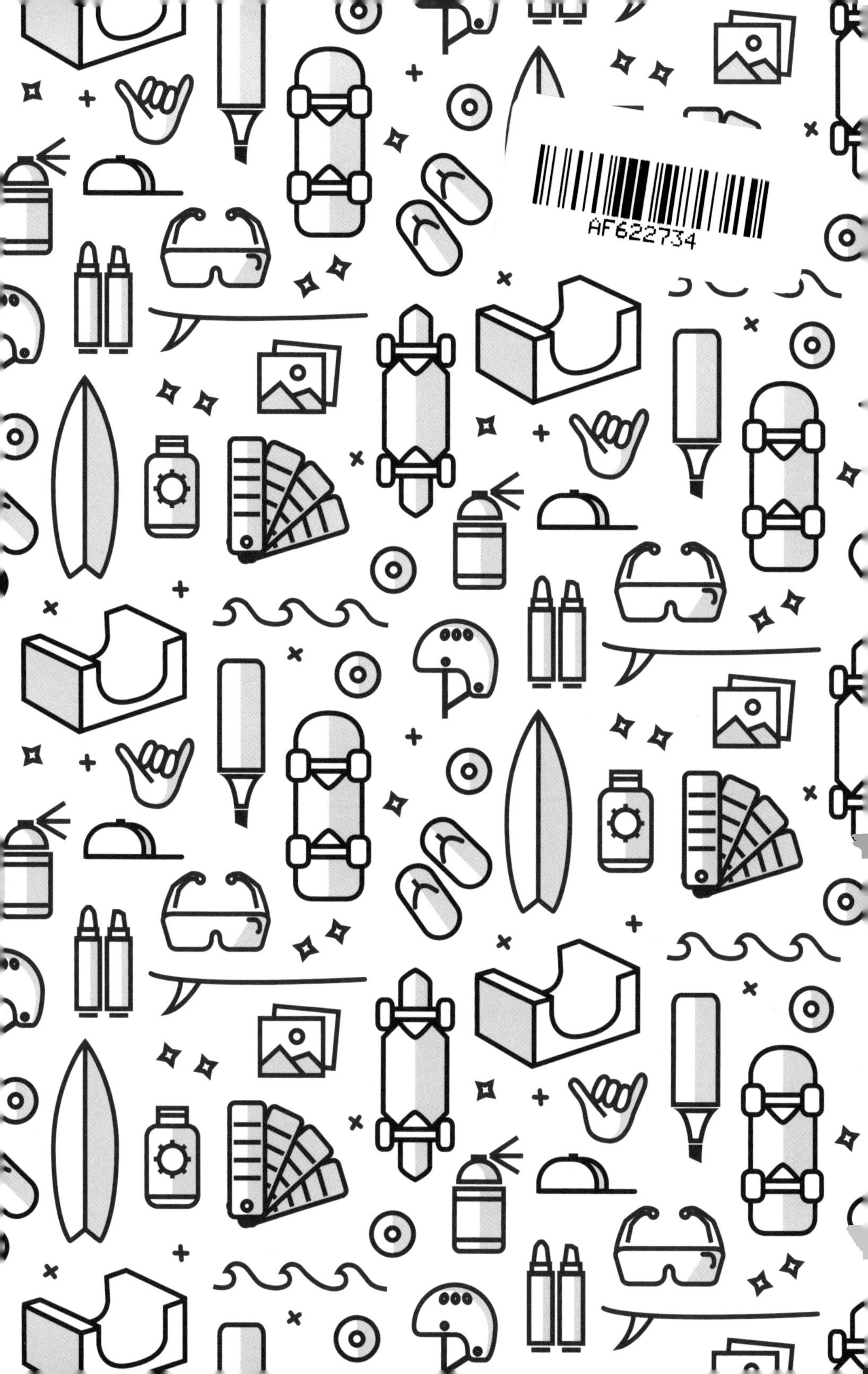

Skate, Surf & Art

Editor, concept, and project director
Anna Minguet

Project's selection, design and layout
Carolina Amell (Monsa Publications)
Cover design
Carolina Amell (Monsa Publications)
Introduction and text edition
Monsa Publications

Cover image & back cover by Andrés de León

INSTITUTO MONSA DE EDICIONES
Gravina 43 (08930)
Sant Adrià de Besòs
Barcelona (Spain)
Tlf. +34 93 381 00 50
www.monsa.com
monsa@monsa.com

ISBN: 978-84-16500-43-7
D.L. B 1787-2017
Printed by Cachiman

BY CAROLINA AMELL

SKATE SURF & ART

monsa

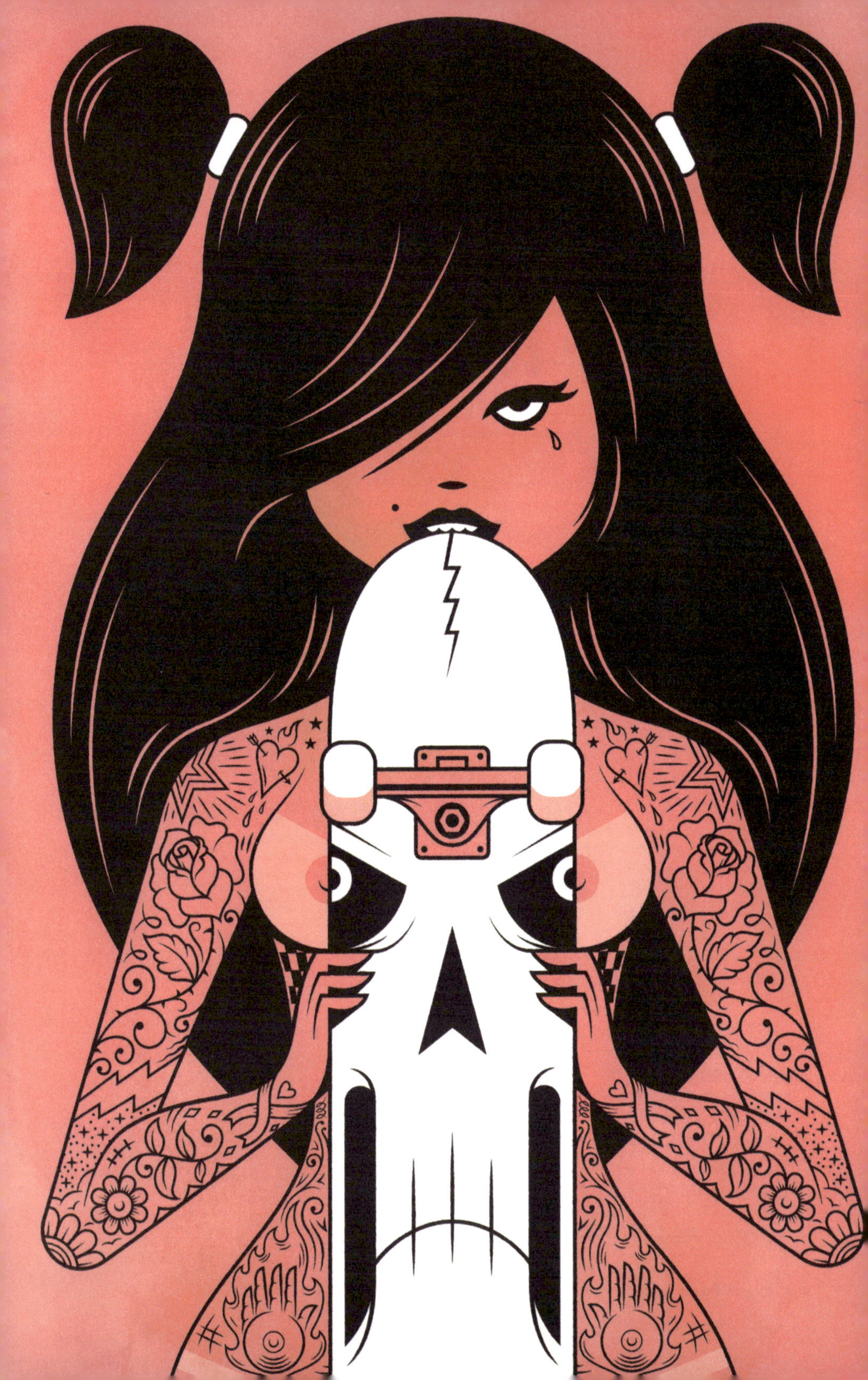

Intro

This extreme sport originated in California USA in the 60's and 70's when the surfing craze was at its height. The idea was to adapt the sport onto land and be able to surf on wheels. The early designs were a simple board customized using roller skate wheels. By 1972 more technologically advanced "skateboards" were appearing on the market. Gradually it became more widespread with its own specialist magazines and media coverage. By the 1980's skateboarding had reached all corners of the USA and was becoming popular worldwide with kids adopting the culture as their own and taking over public spaces to practice the sport.

Over the following pages we will show the work of 44 artists, displaying the evolution of the skateboard with a whole range of designs, colours and shapes. As well as the work they have personally selected for the book, we present an introduction of each one and details of their websites.

The popularity of this sport has grown to such a level that on the 3rd August 2016 the International Olympic Committee voted to include skateboarding as an event for the 2020 Tokyo Olympics. So polish down your board and get ready to enjoy the spectacle.

Este deporte extremo surgió en el estado de California USA entre los años 60 y 70, años en los que el surfing gozaba de miles de seguidores. El motivo principal fue adaptar esa diversión a la tierra, y así poder "surfear" sobre ruedas. Los primeros diseños de estas tablas consistían en sólo un pedazo de madera cualquiera, alterado con ruedas de patines principalmente. Luego, en el año 1972 se comenzó a fabricar "skateboards" con una tecnología más avanzada y específica para esa modalidad. Poco a poco, este movimiento comenzó a destacar en diferentes revistas y medios de comunicación. Ya en los años 80 el "skateboarding" estaba expandido por cada rincón de Estados Unidos, la juventud adquirió esta cultura como suya, al igual que los espacios públicos para poder practicar.

A través de las siguientes páginas, podremos ver los trabajos de 44 artistas, mostrando la evolución del skate en diferentes diseños, colores, y formas. Encontraremos información sobre ellos, así como su sitio web, y veremos los trabajos que han seleccionado especialmente para el libro.

Es tal la afición por este deporte que el 3 de agosto de 2016, el Comité Olímpico Internacional aprobó la incorporación del skateboard para los próximos Juegos Olímpicos de Tokio 2020. Así que saquen brillo a sus tablas y disfruten del espectáculo.

Illustration by **Studio Kronk** // @studiokronk // www.studiokronk.com

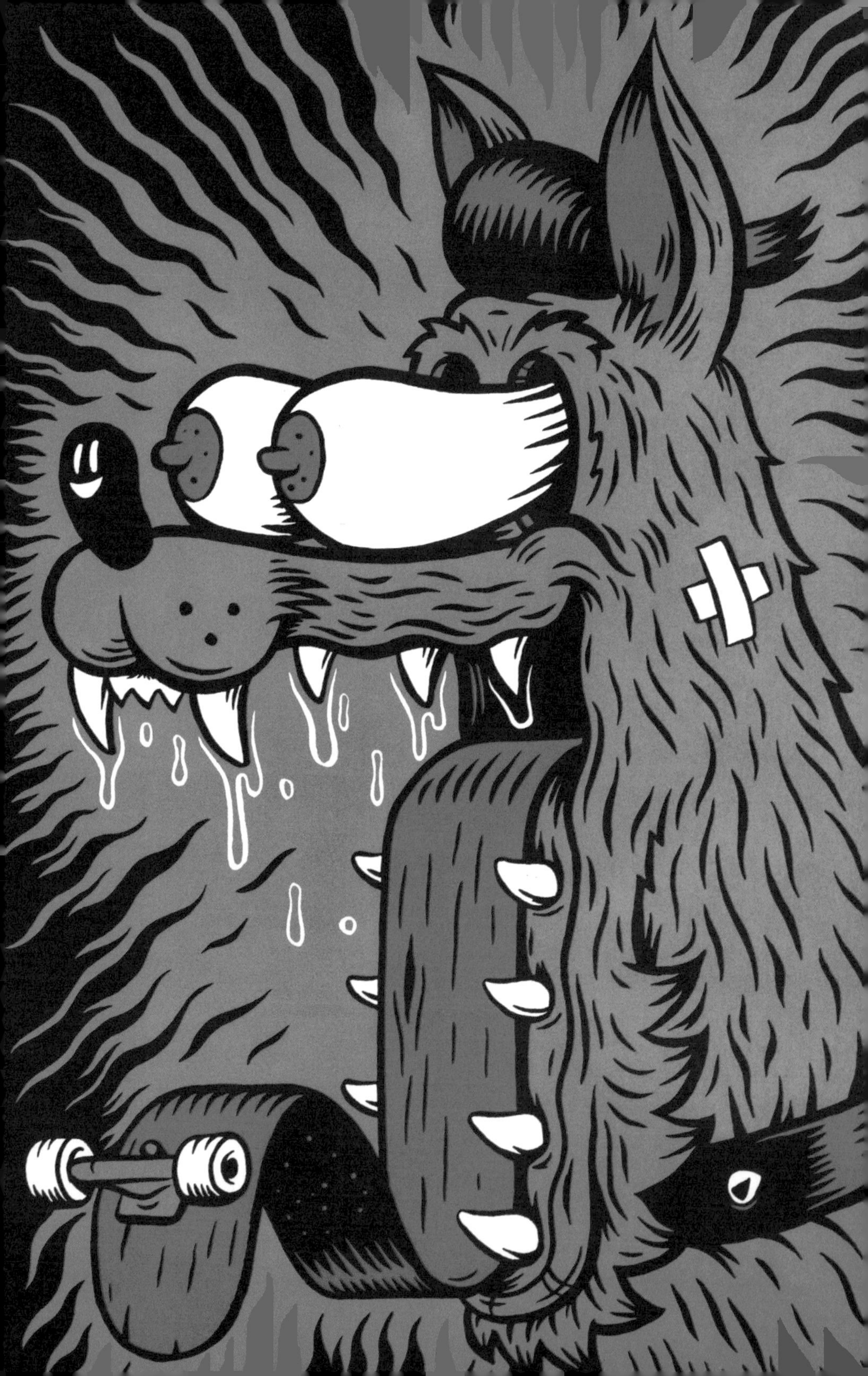

Index

Illustration by **Studio Kronk** // @studiokronk // www.studiokronk.com

Adrian Forrow

www.adrianforrow.com	instagram: @adrian_forrow

Adrian Forrow is a Toronto based, multidisciplinary Artist. Adrian work Celebrates the Simple forms with playful communication.

SkateBoarding Culture has been a major influence on his work from designing his skateboard graphics as a youth, to his professional career as an artist. Adrian finds inspiration in the simplicity of overlooked, odd, and imperfect elements of our culture and tries to visually celebrate them with imagination and charm.

Adrian Forrow es un artista multidisciplinar con sede en Toronto. Consigue crear una comunicación muy divertida utilizando una base siempre de formas simples.

La cultura del SkateBoarding ha sido una gran influencia en su trabajo desde su juventud en el diseño de sus gráficos de skateboard y en la evolución de su carrera profesional como artista. Adrian encuentra inspiración en la simplicidad de elementos olvidados, extraños e imperfectos de nuestra cultura y trata de transmitirlos visualmente con imaginación y encanto.

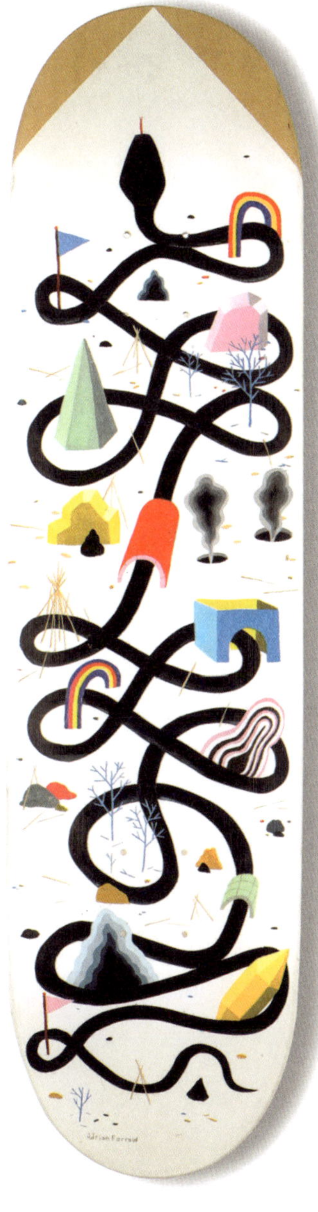

Snake Run // by Adrian Forrow

A piece about exploration and finding the unexpected

Axel Peemoeller

axelpeemoeller.com

Axel Peemoeller works and lives in New York City, his work is driven by design and ideas.

Axel Peemoeller trabaja y vive en New York City, su trabajo es impulsado por el diseño y las ideas.

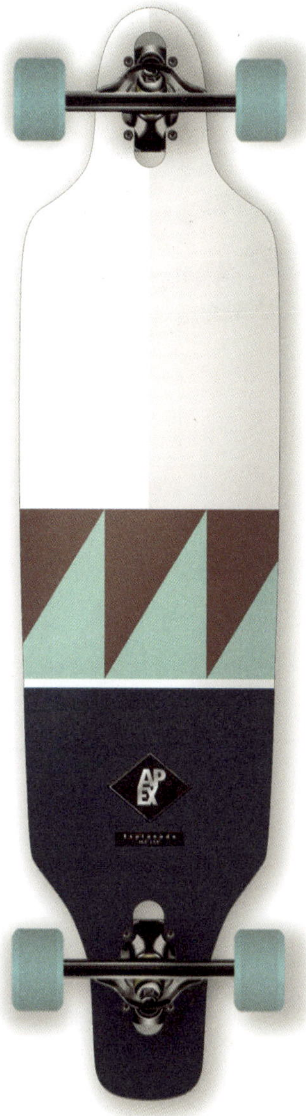

13

by Axel Peemoeller // for APEX Longboards

For the identity and design of the APEX longboards I drew inspiration of bauhaus shapes and nautical flags.

14

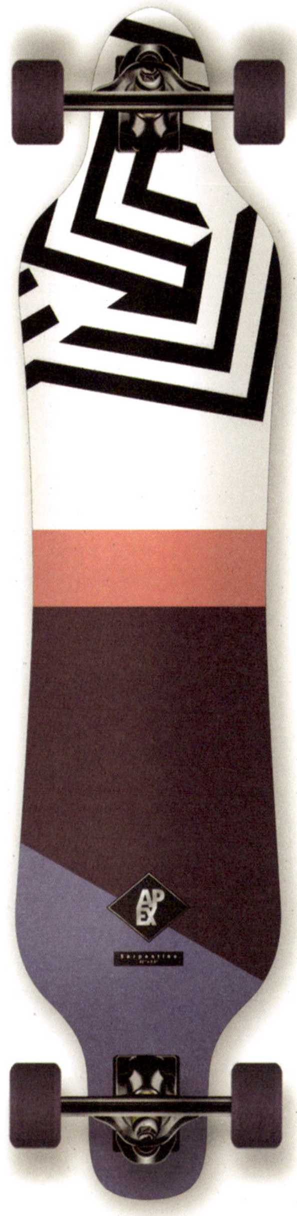

by Axel Peemoeller // for APEX Longboards

by Axel Peemoeller // for APEX Longboards

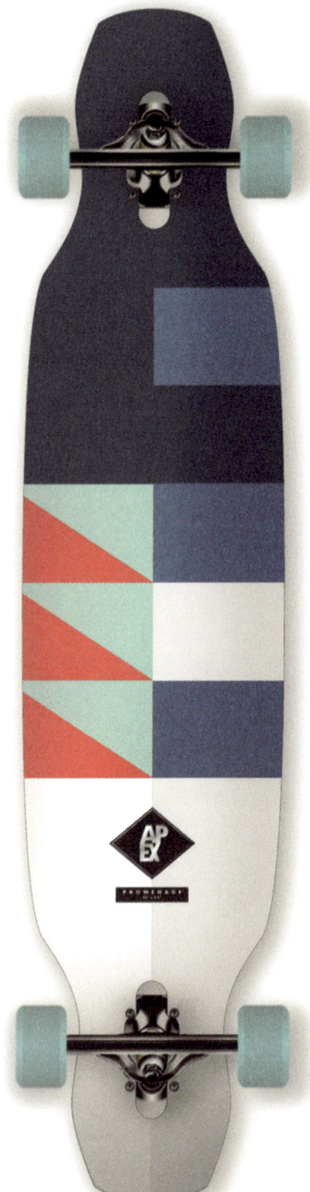

by Axel Peemoeller // for APEX Longboards

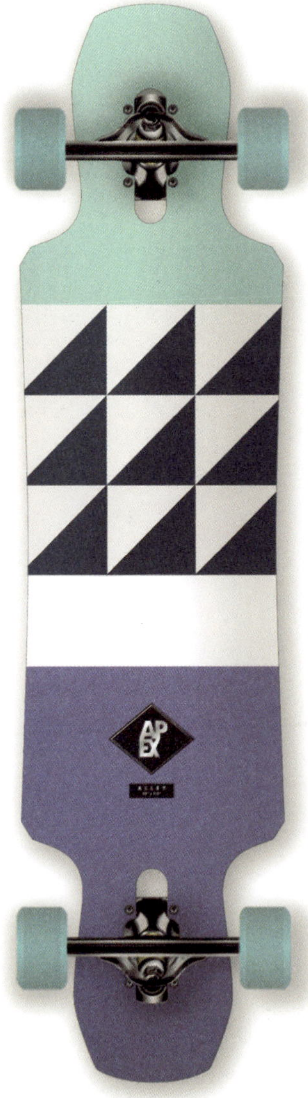

by Axel Peemoeller // for APEX Longboards

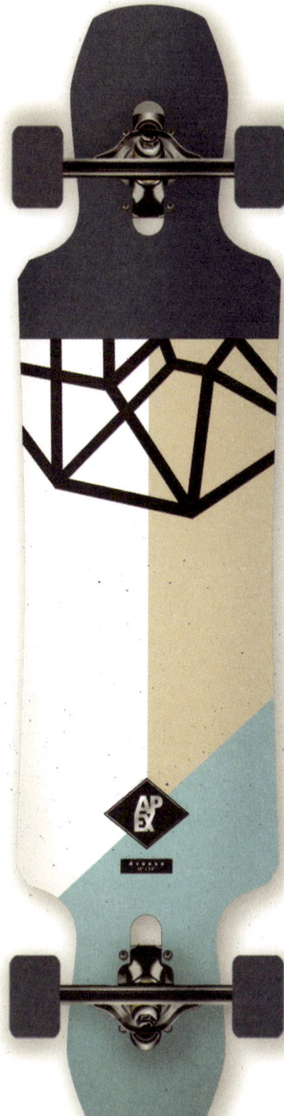

by Axel Peemoeller // for APEX Longboards

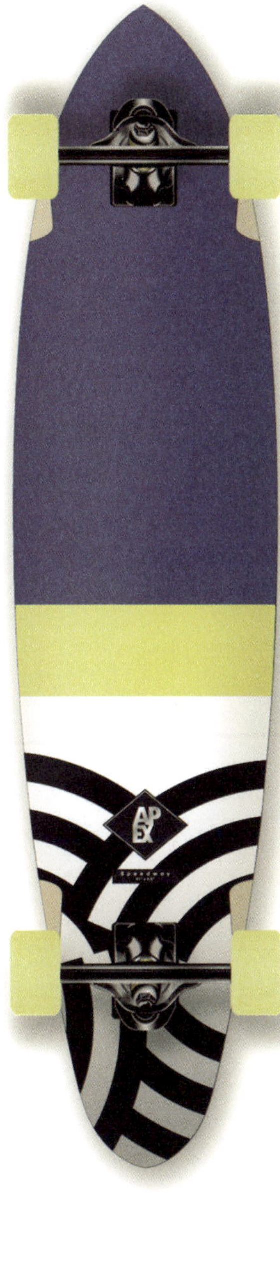

19

by Axel Peemoeller // for APEX Longboards

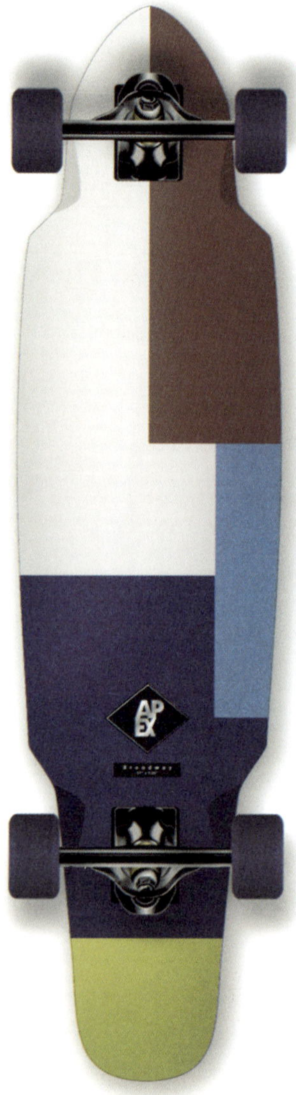

by Axel Peemoeller // for APEX Longboards

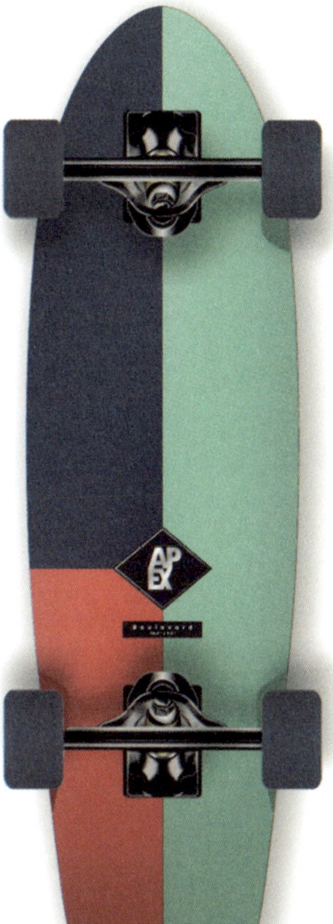

by Axel Peemoeller // for APEX Longboards

Stephanie Abdallah

cargocollective.com/stephanieabdallah

Stephanie Abdallah is an illustrator from Sweden. In 2015 she graduated from Beckmans College of Design with a BFA in Visual Communication.

She works mostly with traditional mediums and she is most loyal to the good old pen and paper. Stephanie strives to make beautiful and intricate designs that make the eye wander. She wants the viewer to always find something new when they look at a drawing.

Stephanie is inspired by nature, science, dreams and psychology.

Stephanie Abdallah es una ilustradora de Suecia. En 2015 se graduó en "Beckmans College of Design" con un "BFA" en Comunicación Visual. Trabaja principalmente con herramientas tradicionales, ella prefiere su vieja pluma y papel para poder crear.

Stephanie se esfuerza por hacer diseños hermosos y complicados, que despierten sensaciones al observar sus dibujos, ella quiere que el espectador siempre encuentre algo nuevo.

Stephanie se inspira en la naturaleza, la ciencia, los sueños y la psicología.

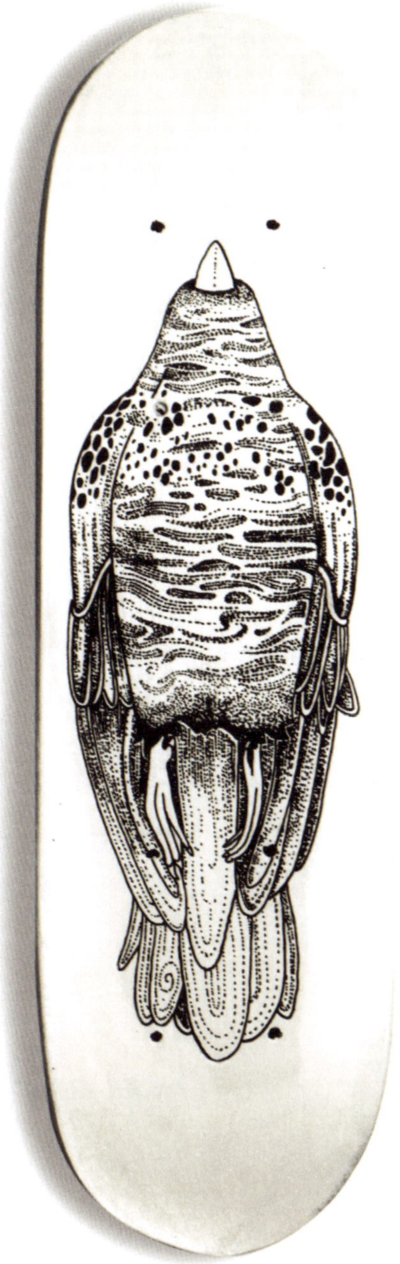

Bird Deck // by Stephanie Abdallah

A triptych of birds. Done with pen on skateboards.

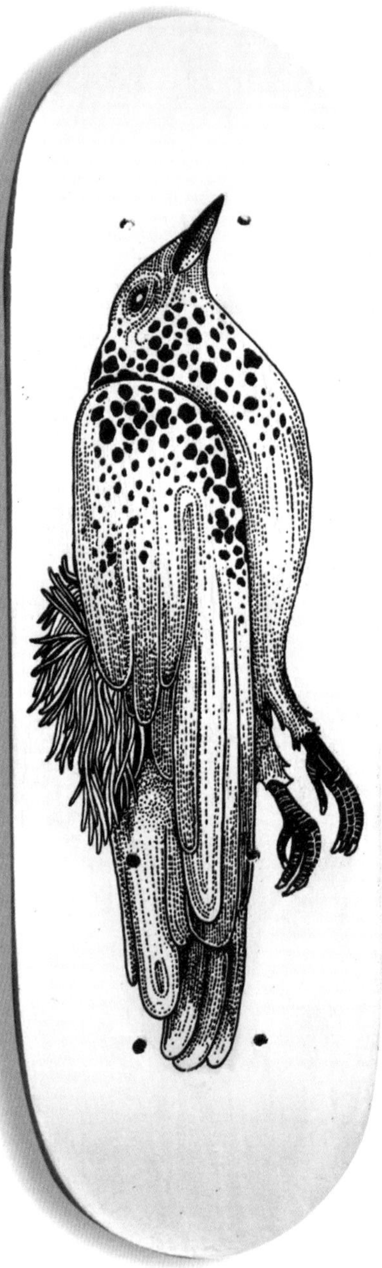

Bird Deck // by Stephanie Abdallah

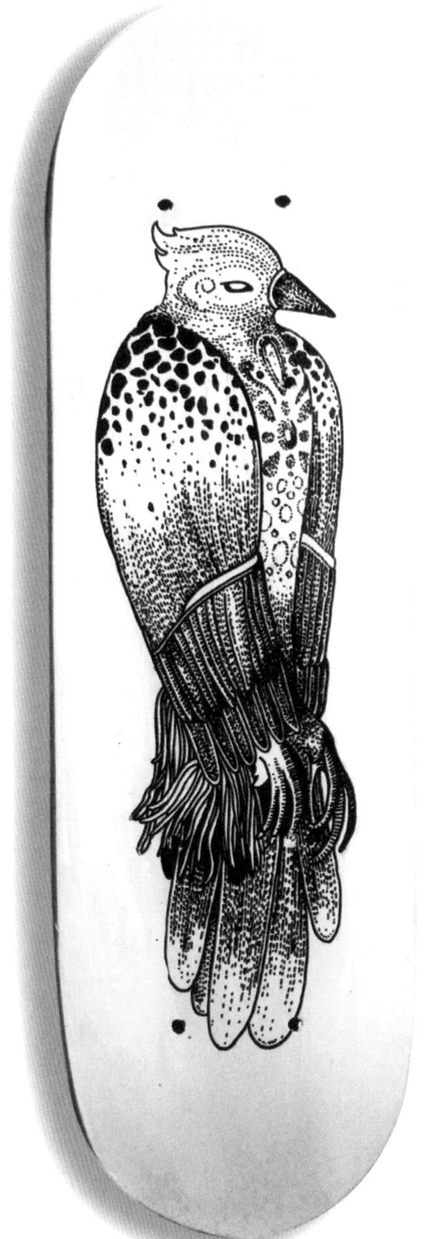

Bird Deck // by Stephanie Abdallah

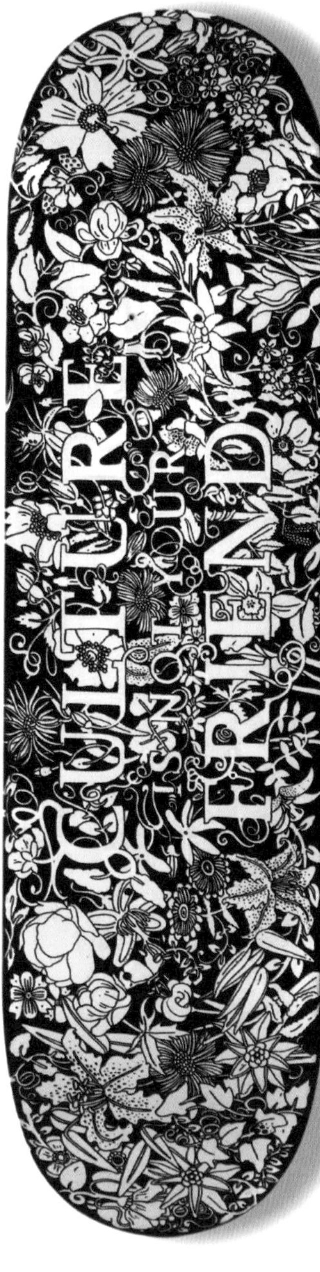

Culture is not your friend // by Stephanie Abdallah

"Culture is not your friend" is a quote by Terrence McKenna that inspires me. Done with acrylics and markers.

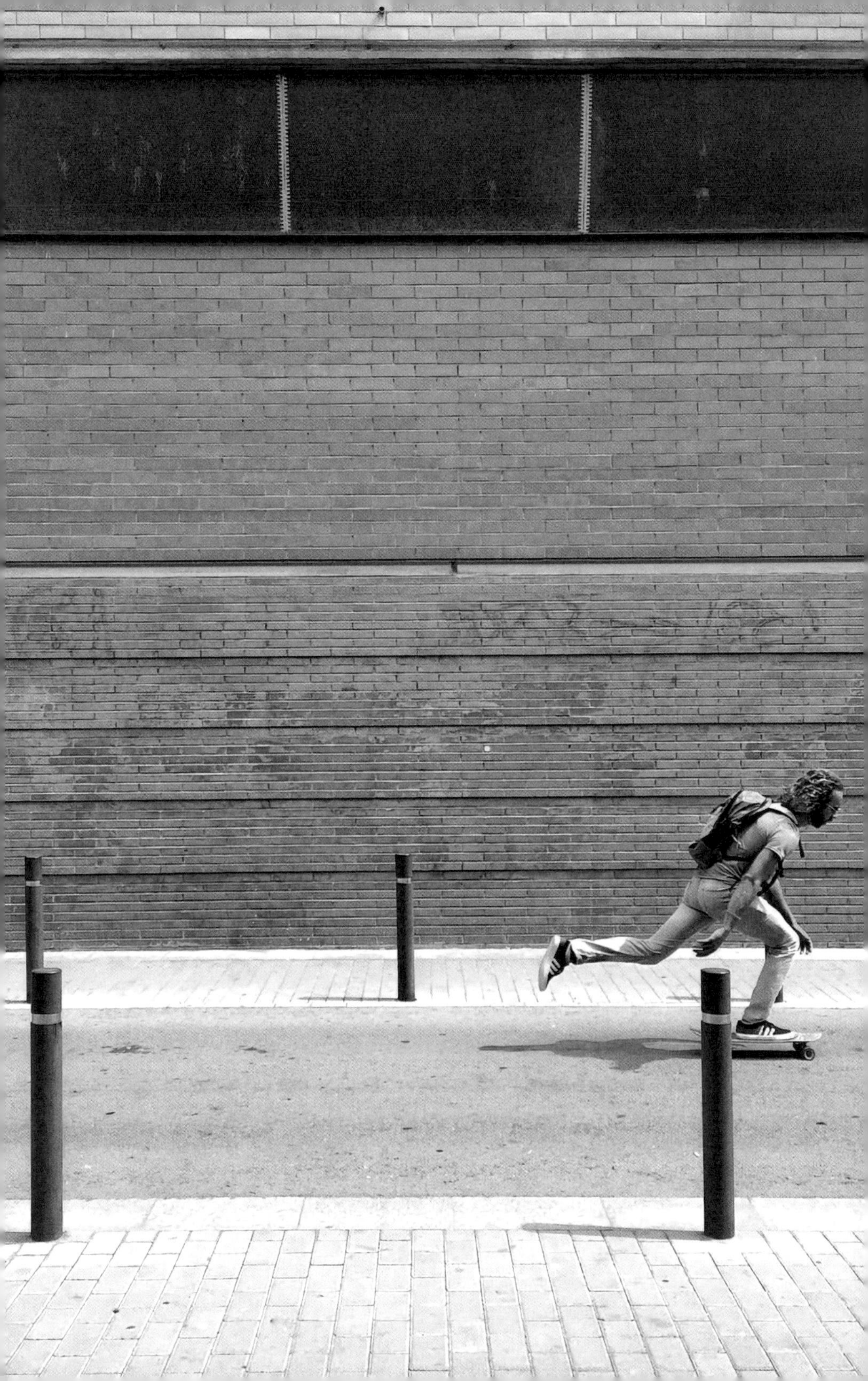

Fakir

fakirdesign.com

Olivier Gonthier aka Fakir, founder of a freelance studio called Fakirdesign wich is based in Paris, France.

Olivier has more than one string in his bow: he is painter, illustrator and toy designer. He also practises graffiti, uses illustrator and photoshop, but in general he adapts the technique to each project and the medium.

A big part of Olivier's work is inspired by Japanese culture which fascinates him, and his favorite themes are Asian food and bestiary. He also likes to reinterpret, "diverting" famous icon, or characters of his childhood.

Olivier Gonthier alias Fakir, fundador de un estudio freelance llamado Fakirdesign que tiene su sede en París, Francia.

Olivier tiene más de una cuerda en su arco: es pintor, ilustrador y diseñador de juguetes. También practica el graffiti, usa illustrator y photoshop, pero en general adapta la técnica a cada proyecto y al medio.

Una gran parte del trabajo de Olivier se inspira en la cultura japonesa que le fascina, y sus temas favoritos son la comida asiática y el bestiario. También le gusta reinterpretar, famosos iconos o personajes de su infancia.

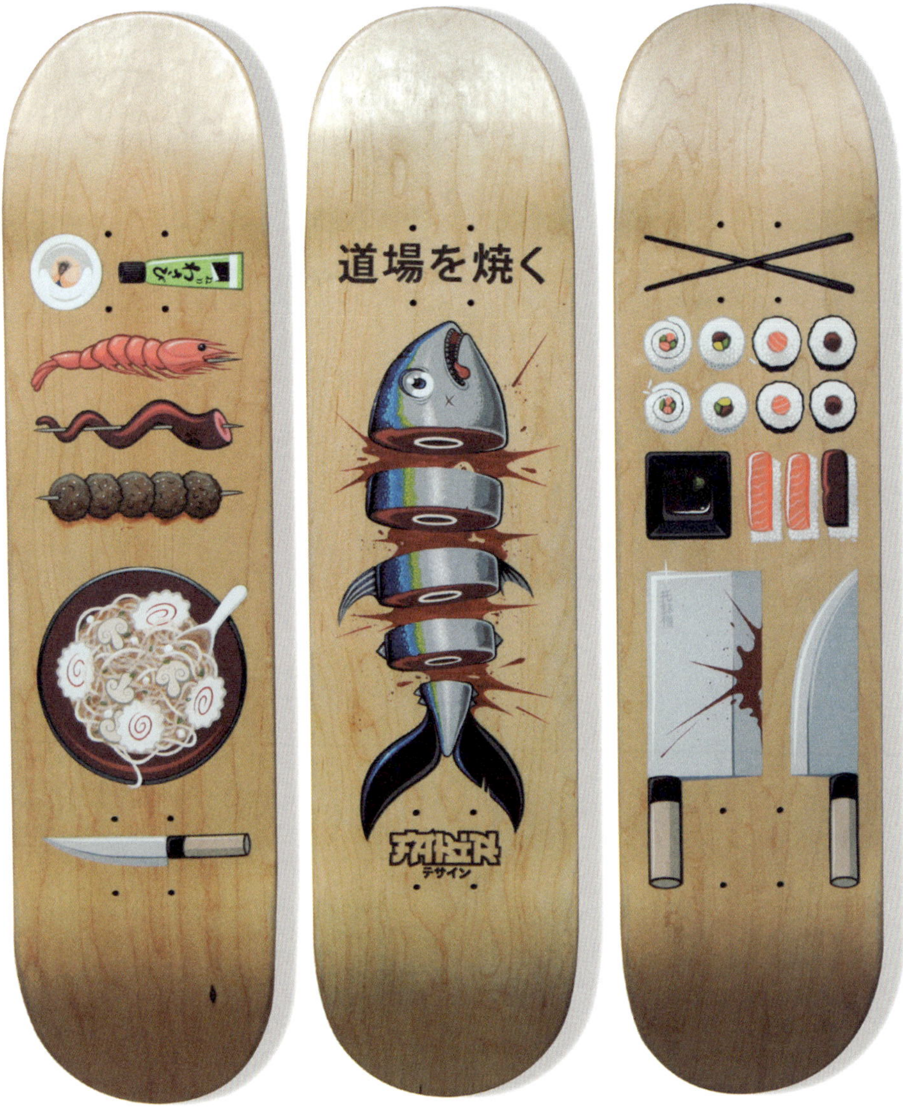

Burning Dojo // by Fakir

This triptych was originally a handpainted custom that has now found its limited edition following the great success he met. Available on Lastconcept.com

RAWRAMIREZ

www.rawramirez.com	instagram: @Rawramirez

Venezuelan illustrator and Graphic Designer based in Buenos Aires.
His obsession with geometric shapes and powerful colors makes rawramirez's paintings easy to recognize.
Eyes are the distinctive icon of his work.

Rawramirez es un ilustrador venezolano y diseñador gráfico con sede en Buenos Aires.
Su obsesión por las formas geométricas y los potentes colores hacen que sus pinturas sean fáciles de reconocer.
Los ojos son el icono distintivo de su obra.

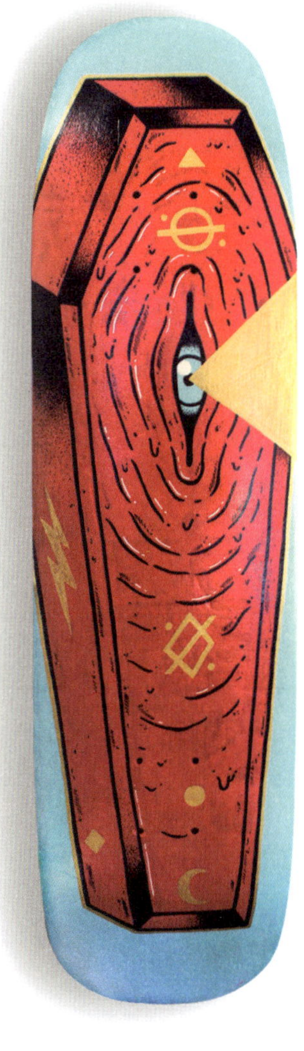

Ataúd // by RAWRAMIREZ

Acrylics, marker, ink

Denis Carrier

www.studiofolk.com

Denis Carrier, looks like his work: not so big, not very muscular, but really funny and simple.
A central idea, clearly introduced, often humourous, always effective.
No twirl or flourish, his illustrations are hand made or use vector techniques: and that works! Somewhere between naivety and a strange world, you're of course welcome!

Denis Carrier, se parece a su trabajo: no tan grande y musculoso, pero realmente divertido y simple.
En sus trabajos siempre existe una idea central, claramente introducida, a menudo chistosa, y muy eficaz. Sus ilustraciones suelen estar hechas a mano o utilizando técnicas de vectores. ¡y eso funciona! En algún lugar entre la ingenuidad y un mundo extraño, ¡por supuesto que eres bienvenido!

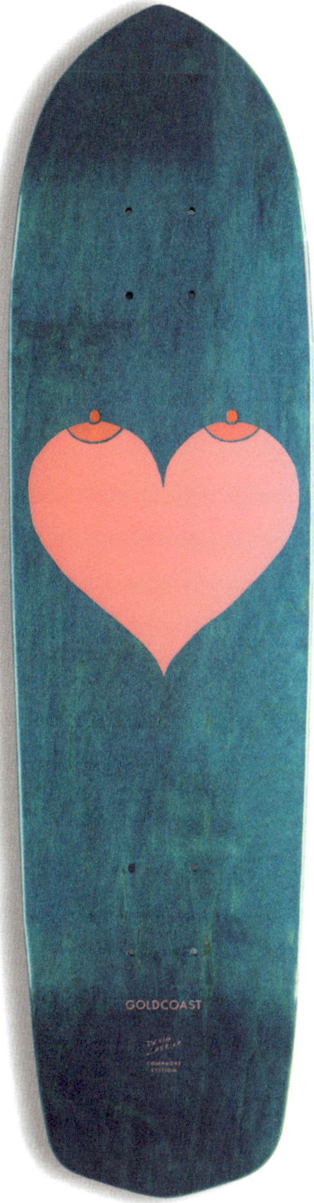

GoldCoast HeartOn // by Denis Carrier

This was a Compadre Edition collaboration project between GoldCoast and French illustrator Denis Carrier. The simplicity of the message is the beauty.

Guillermo Trapiello

guillermotrapiello.com	guillermotrapiello.blogspot.com.es

Guillermo Trapiello (Madrid, 1985) is a visual artist who graduated in Architecture from the Madrid European University (Madrid, 2012).

He is also the editor of Negocios Raros, creator of walkwithmemaps, member of Naciónrotonda and a cartographer for the National Geographic.

He currently runs his own Madrid office where he works on peripheral architecture, from the design stage through to the production of installations and furniture.

Guillermo Trapiello (Madrid, 1985) es artista visual y licenciado en arquitectura por la Universidad Europea de Madrid (Madrid, 2012).

También es editor en Negocios Raros, creador de walkwithmemaps, miembro de Naciónrotonda y cartógrafo en National Geographic.

En la actualidad dirige su oficina en Madrid desde la que desarrolla trabajos de arquitectura periférica, desde el diseño editorial hasta la producción de instalaciones y mobiliario.

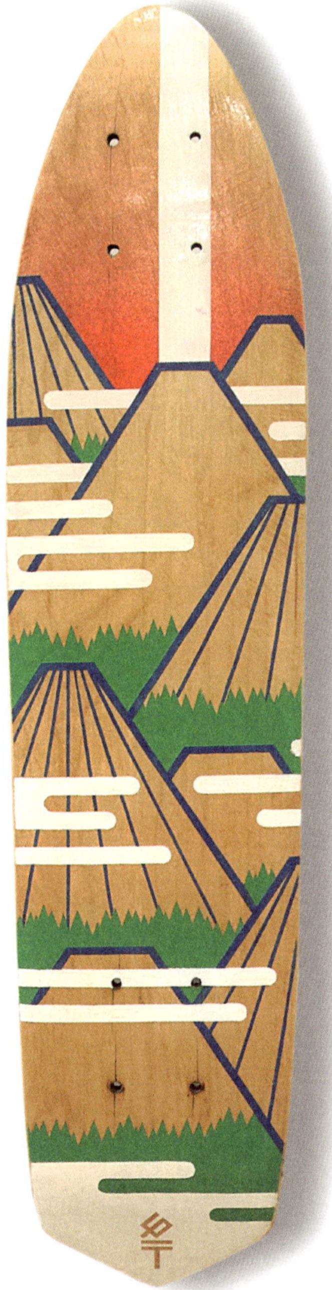

Reclaimed skateboard // by Guillermo Trapiello

Acrylic paint on wood.

Geoffrey Holstad

geoffreyholstad.com

Geoffrey Holstad (b. 1986, Michigan, USA) is a plein air graphic designer, printmaker, citizen meteorologist, birdwatcher, and morning person. He is a subscriber to a strong fun ethic, simplicity, chips & salsa, lake surfing, always ever optimism, instant coffee, christmas music, reading out loud, homemade haircuts, and the snow belt.

Geoffrey Holstad (1986, Michigan, Estados Unidos) es un diseñador gráfico al aire libre, printmaker, ciudadano meteorólogo, observador de aves y persona diurna. Él es un suscriptor con una fuerte ética de la diversión, la sencillez, las chips & salsa, el surf en el lago, el optimismo, el café instantáneo, la música de Navidad, la lectura en voz alta, los cortes de cabello caseros y el cinturón de nieve.

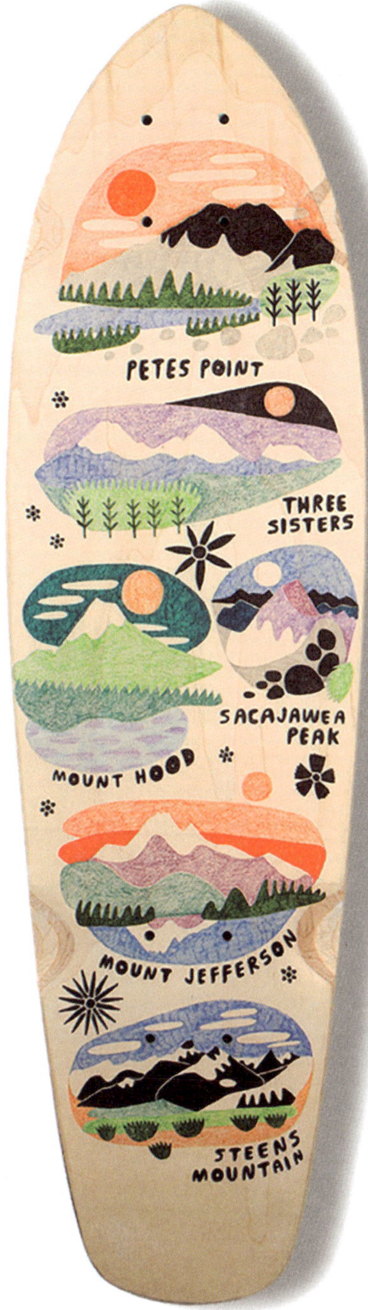

Peaks of Oregon // by Geoffrey Holstad

Chio Romero

www.chioromero.com

Graphic artist / illustrator / design-addicted who loves simplistic design and detailed illustration.

Chio Romero's work range includes: editorial illustration, branding, typography, photography, poster illustration and graphic design.

He likes to deal with his projects as something unique and genuine in order to give an individualized response to each of them. Chio loves to experiment with ink lettering, calligraphy and craft and applying them in his projects. All his work tries to be a blend of life experiences, music, tradition and a lot of hard work.

Artista gráfico / ilustrador / diseño-adicto que ama el diseño simplista y la ilustración detallada.

La gama de trabajo de Chio Romero incluye: ilustración editorial, branding, tipografía, fotografía, ilustración de carteles y diseño gráfico.

Le gusta tratar sus proyectos como algo único y genuino para dar una respuesta individualizada a cada uno de ellos. A Chio le encanta experimentar con letras de tinta, caligrafía y artesanía y aplicarlas en sus proyectos. Todo su trabajo trata de ser una mezcla de experiencias de vida, música, tradición y trabajo duro.

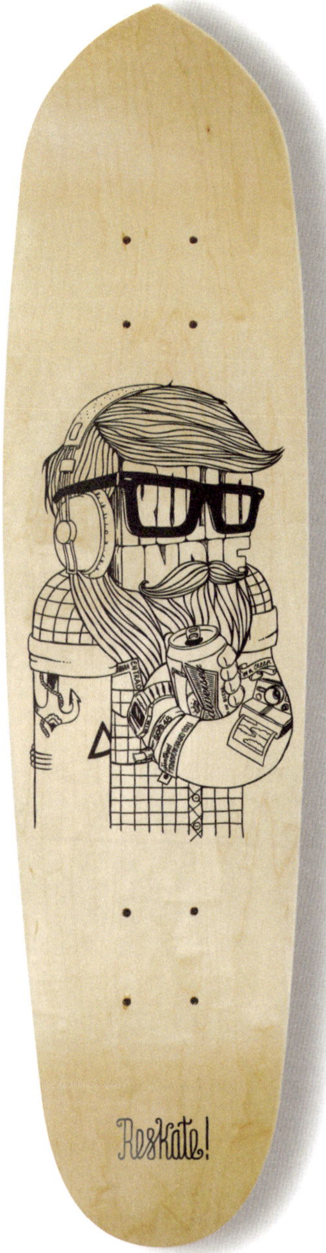

Rollo Indie // by Chio Romero

Illustration inspired by the drummer of one of Chio's favourite bands: "Los Planetas".
It is a mash of indie-culture stereotypes and what I hate about the "anti-mainstream era".

JMYES

www.jesusmorenoyes.com

The work of Jesús Moreno 'Yes' is based on a geometric language from which he creates sets of lines, coloured figures and tangents which evoke ancient symbolism and alphabets. With links to his past in the graffiti field, Yes starts with letters, characters and words which are then taken to an abstract level making the initial script unrecognizable. In addition his works focuses on the search for the ideal spot in which to begin, as this often fires the creative process.

His passion for discovering new cultures and locations has led him to paint and exhibit in countries from Spain to Mexico, Bolivia, Portugal and Thailand. He is currently represented by the Slowtrack gallery.

El trabajo de Jesús Moreno 'Yes' se desarrolla a través de un lenguaje geométrico del que obtiene juegos de líneas, figuras coloristas y tangencias que remiten a simbología antigua y diferentes alfabetos. Conectando con su inicio en la creación plástica, el graffiti, Yes parte de letras, caracteres y palabras que abstrae hasta el punto de casi no poder reconocer lo que se escribió en un principio. Por otro lado, su labor destaca por la búsqueda del spot, del lugar adecuado para intervenir, ya que a menudo es este el que enciende su proceso creativo.

Su afán por descubrir nuevas culturas y lugares le ha llevado tanto a pintar como a exponer en diferentes países como España, México, Bolivia, Portugal o Tailandia. Actualmente está representado por la galería Slowtrack.

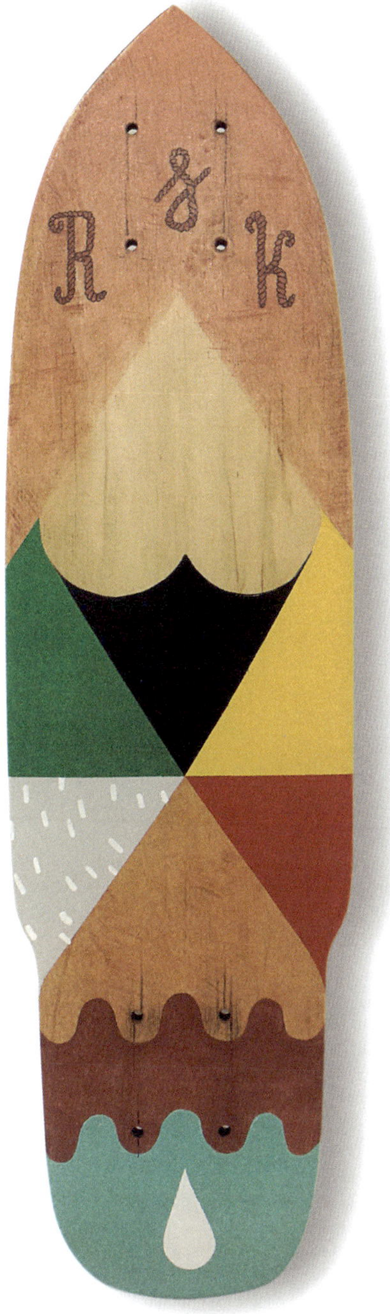

by JMYES

Kate O'Hara

kate-ohara.com

Kate O'Hara is a freelance illustrator currently living in Reno, Nevada. She graduated from the Illustration program at the University of the Arts in Philadelphia, in 2014. She creates nature inspired illustrations that draw people in through their nostalgic mood and intricate detail. She often uses interactions between plants, animals and their environment as concepts to illustrate human behavior.

Kate O'Hara es un ilustrador independiente que actualmente vive en Reno, Nevada. Se graduó en el programa de ilustración de la Universidad de las Artes de Filadelfia, en 2014. Crea ilustraciones inspiradas en la naturaleza que atraen a la gente a través de su estado de ánimo nostálgico y sus complejos detalles. Utiliza a menudo las interacciones entre las plantas, los animales y su ambiente como conceptos para ilustrar el comportamiento humano.

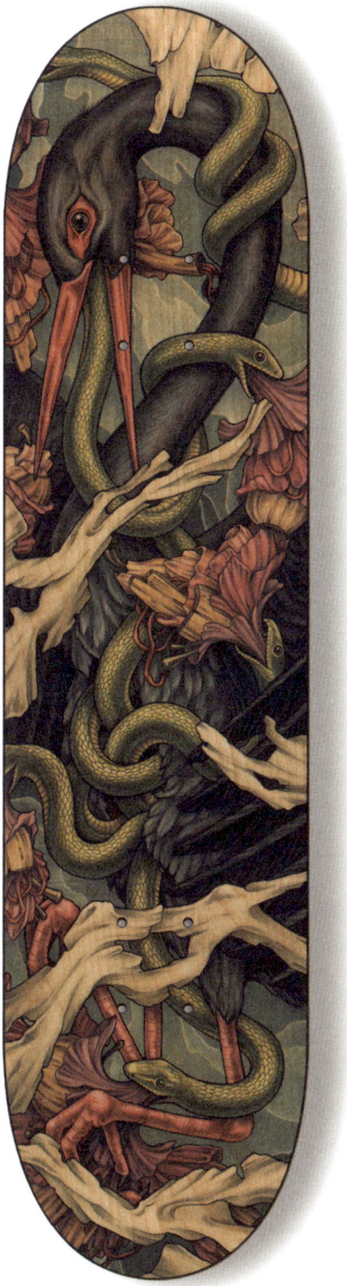

Harbinger // by Kate O'Hara

A skateboard design for Light Grey Art Lab's show, 'Skate or Die.'

Keith Negley

www.keithnegley.com

Keith Negley is a nationally recognized illustrator and author hailing from the mountains of Bellingham Washington. He is a frequent contributor to The New York Times and New Yorker and his work has appeared on everything from book covers and album covers to skateboard decks and watches. He has been awarded four medals from the Society of Illustrators over his career, and has been featured in annuals such as *American Illustration*, and *Communication Arts*.

Keith Negley es un ilustrador reconocido nacionalmente y autor procedente de las montañas de Bellingham Washington. Él es un colaborador frecuente de The New York Times y New Yorker y su trabajo lo puedes encontrar desde portadas de libros y portadas de discos hasta tablas de skate y relojes. Ha sido galardonado con cuatro medallas de la Sociedad de Ilustradores a lo largo de su carrera, y ha sido presentado en anuarios como el de American Illustration, y el de Artes de la Comunicación.

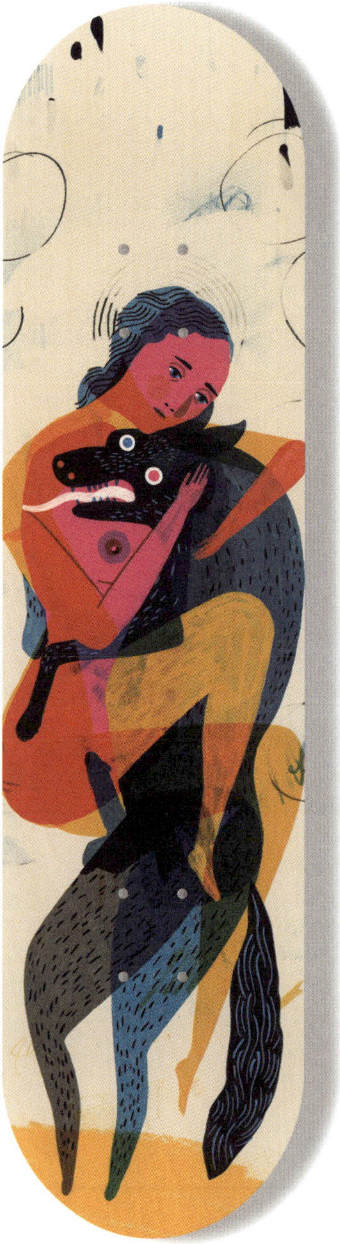

45

by Keith Negley

Michael Nÿkamp

mkn-design.com	instagram: @mkn_design

Michael Nÿkamp is a designer and illustrator born and raised in Ontario, Canada. His only complaint (politely filed, of course) is that there are never enough pencils in the office. He strives to make the complex simple and the simple beautiful through illustrative design to elevate brands.

Michael Nÿkamp es un diseñador e ilustrador nacido y criado en Ontario, Canadá. Su única queja (cortésmente archivada, por supuesto) es que nunca hay suficientes lápices en la oficina. Él se esfuerza por hacer que el complejo sea simple y lo simple hermoso a través de un diseño ilustrativo para elevar las marcas.

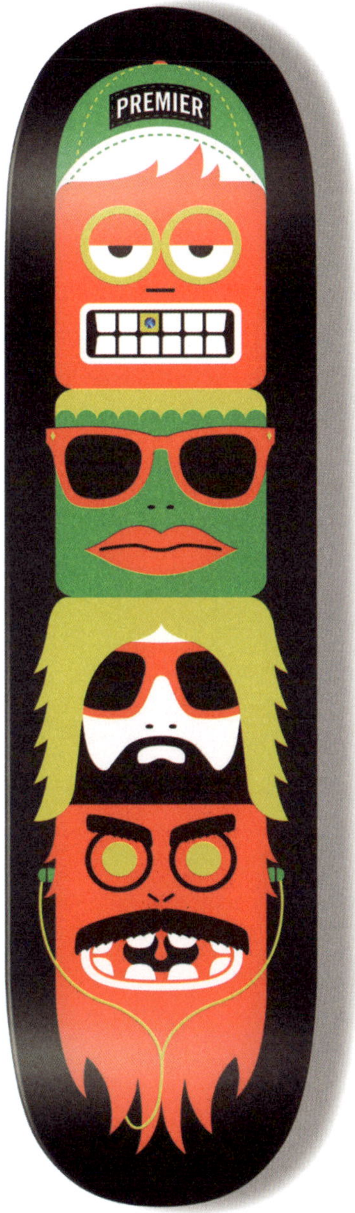

Urban Totem // by Michael Nÿkamp

This deck illustration was created for a fundraiser to build a new skatepark.

Scott Albrecht

ScottAlbrecht.com

Currently based in Brooklyn, NY, Scott Albrecht's work is made from a shared interest of art and design, often acting as a distillation of his daily experiences into a his own brand of graphic abstractions.

El trabajo de Scott Albrecht tiene su base actualmente en Brooklyn, Nueva York, a partir de un interés común entre el arte y el diseño, que a menudo actúa como una destilación de sus experiencias cotidianas en una marca propia de abstracciones gráficas.

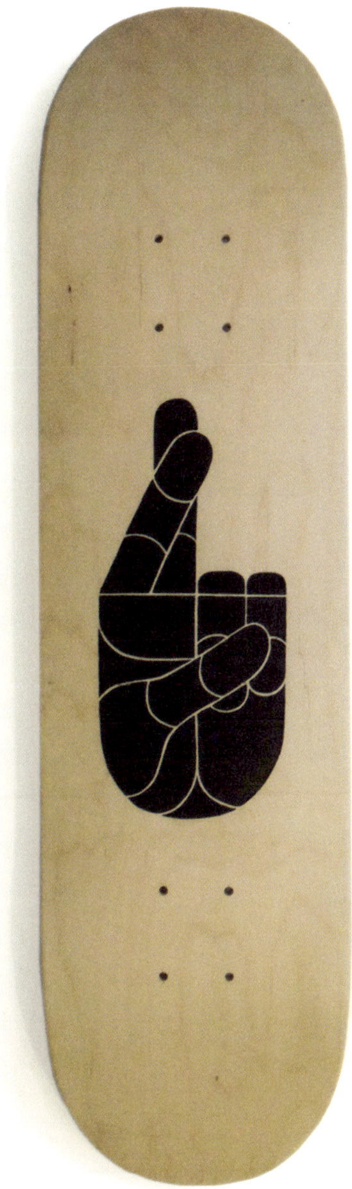

Hopeful // by Scott Albrecht

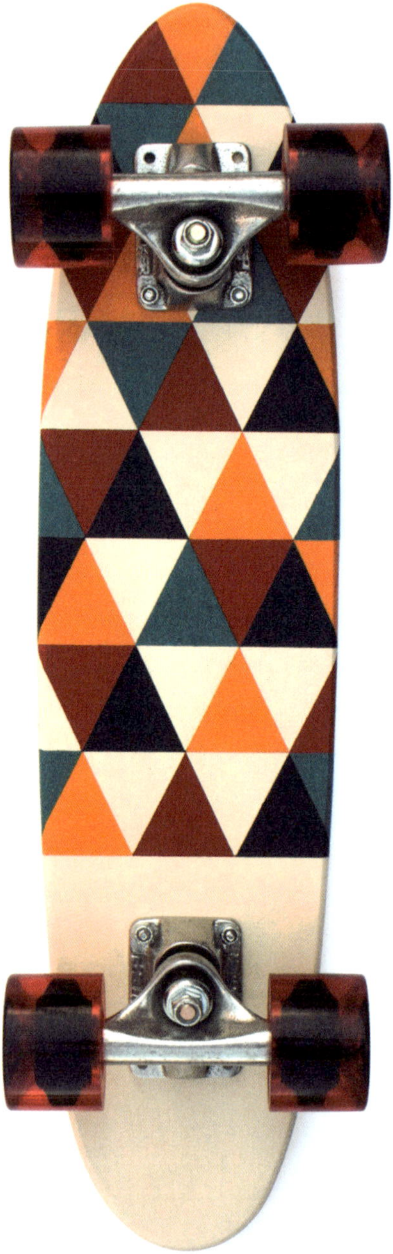

Cruiser No3 // by Scott Albrecht

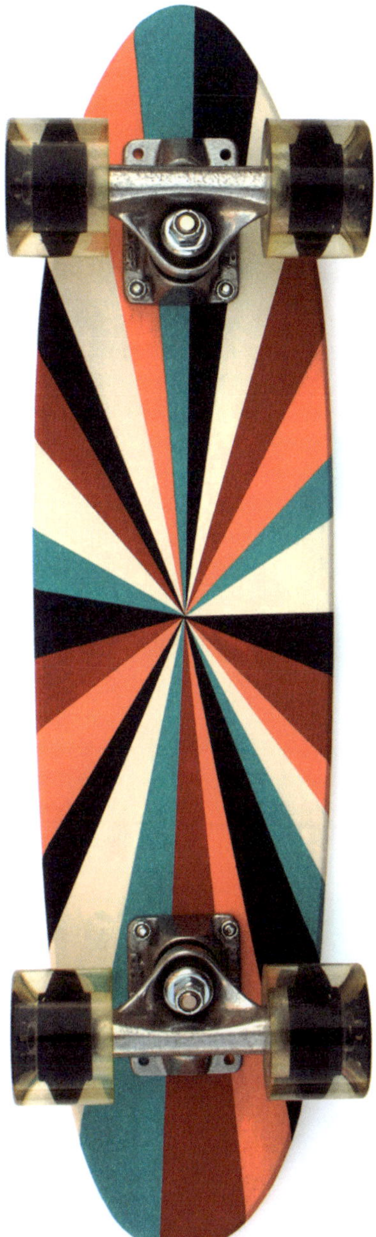

Cruiser No4 // by Scott Albrecht

Ekiem

www.ekiem.com | instagram: @ekiemone

Ekiem is a French freelance artist and graphic designer born near the Parisian suburbs. At an early stage in his career, he developed a keen interest in creative visuals. His style revolves around simplicity, stemming from clear and molded lines, mixing bold colours, repeated patterns and often using type processing. He is constantly searching for new visual combinations and works with a vast array of materials. His work is published through screen prints, t-shirts, stickers and original artworks. Ekiem is a versatile and hard-working visual artist exhibiting his work as often as possible.

Ekiem es un artista freelance francés y diseñador gráfico nacido cerca de los suburbios parisinos. En una etapa temprana de su carrera, desarrolló un gran interés en las imágenes creativas. Su estilo gira en torno a la sencillez, proveniente de líneas claras y moldeadas, mezclando colores en negrita, patrones repetidos y a menudo usando el procesamiento de tipos. Está constantemente buscando nuevas combinaciones visuales y trabaja con una amplia gama de materiales. Su trabajo se publica a través de serigrafías, camisetas, pegatinas y obras de arte originales. Ekiem es un artista visual versátil y trabajador, podemos ver su trabajo exhibido con frecuencia.

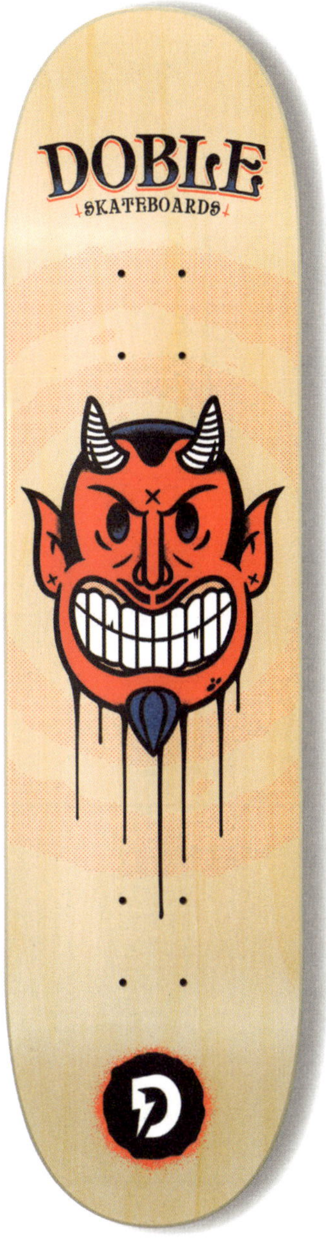

Devil // by Ekiem

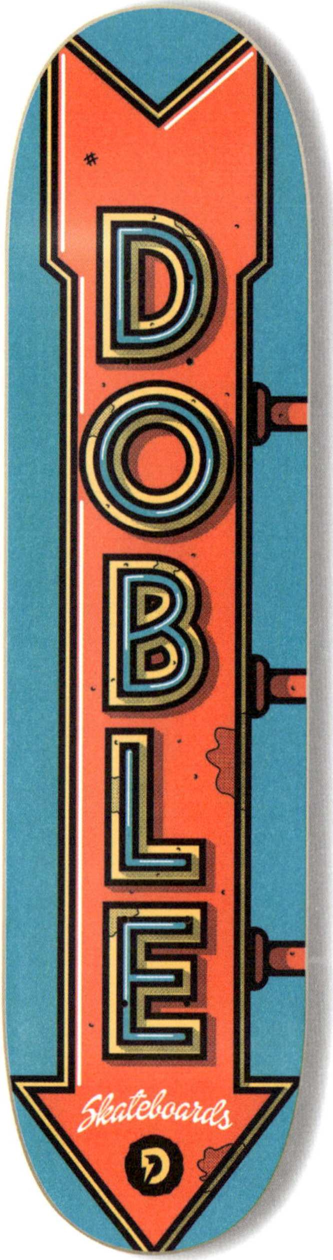

Sign // by Ekiem

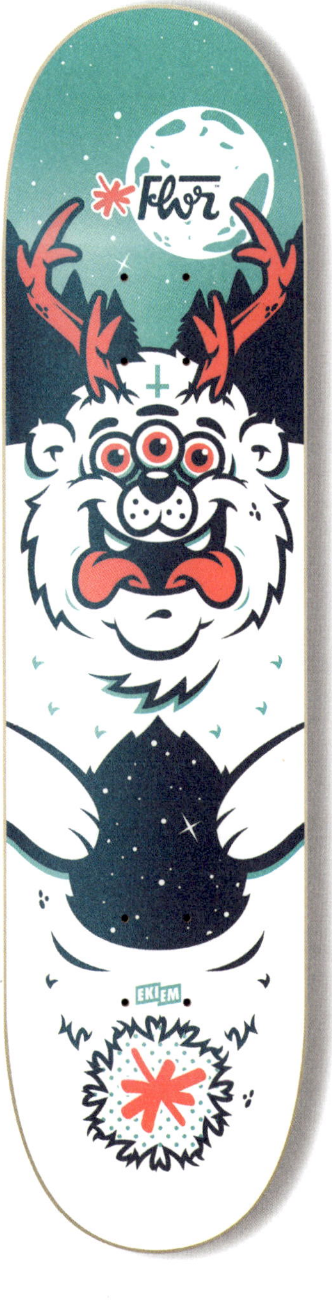

Horned bear // by Ekiem

Esra Roise

www.esraroise.com	instagram: @esrarois

Esra works full-time as a fashion illustrator, but the skate community has been a part of her life ever since her youth, when she would watch skate-movies and spend time in skateparks, with here brother and friends. Years later she got to work for a long time in an Oslo skateshop, and has since 2014 been an official advocate for skatebrand Element Eden.

Esra is based in Oslo, Norway but works with clients worldwide. She is represented by Unit Agency.

Esra trabaja a tiempo completo como ilustradora de moda, pero la comunidad de skate ha sido parte de su vida desde su juventud, a menudo miraba películas de skate y pasaba el tiempo en skateparks, con su hermano y amigos. Años más tarde estuvo trabajado durante mucho tiempo en una tienda de patinaje de Oslo, y desde el año 2014 ha sido una defensora oficial del Element Eden skatebrand.

Esra tiene su base en Oslo, Noruega, pero trabaja con clientes de todo el mundo. Está representada por la Unit Agency.

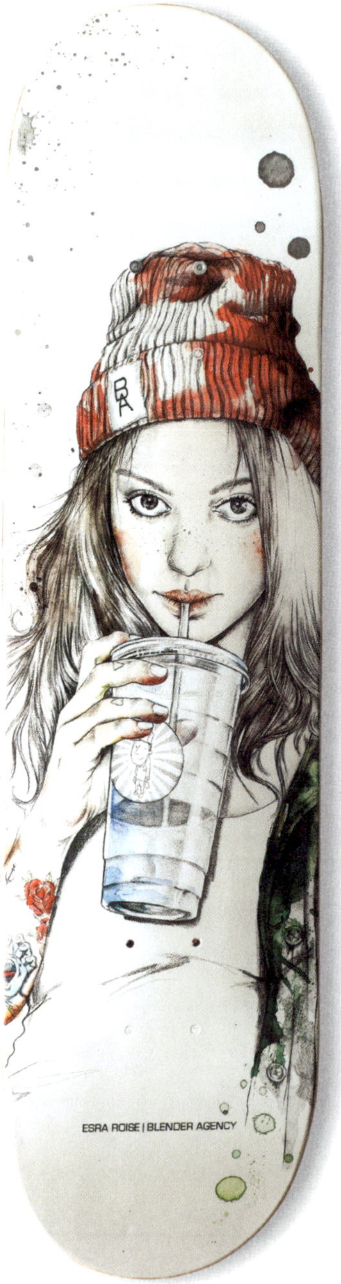

by Esra Roise // for Blender deck

Esra Roise and Blender Agency have know each other for years, and in conjunction with the 10th Anniversary of Blender Agency, they created this limited edition skateboard deck to celebrate.

Gonzalo Ares Villafañe

www.behance.net/GonziAV

Gonzalo is a graphic designer but he loves illustration and animation as well. He used to work in a motion graphic studio for some time but now he is focusing in illustration and developing video games.

Gonzalo es un diseñador gráfico al que le encanta la ilustración y la animación. Trabajó en un estudio gráfico durante algún tiempo, y ahora se está centrando en la ilustración y el desarrollo de videojuegos.

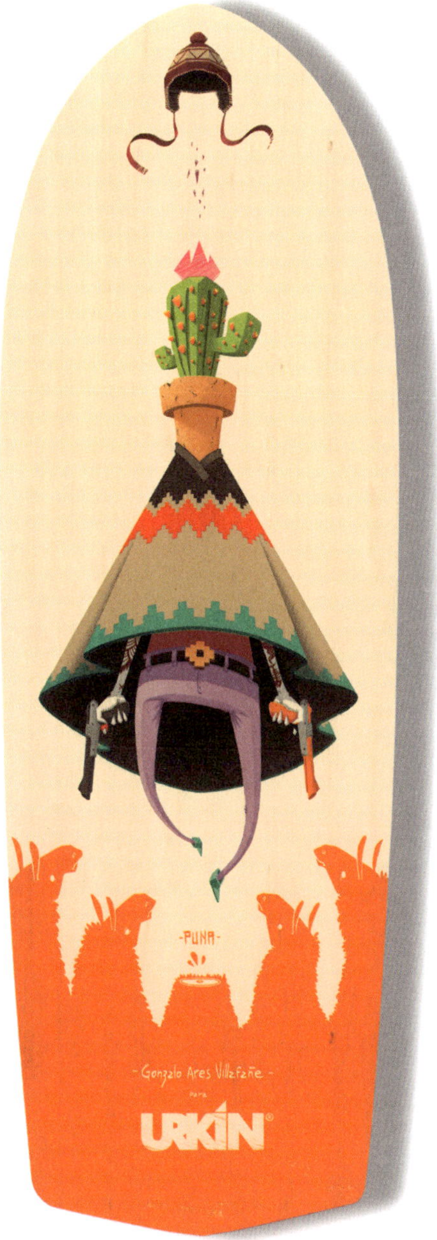

Puna // Gonzalo Ares Villafañe // for Urkin skateboards

Kinga Offert

www.offert.com.pl

Kinga Offert is an artist, illustrator and print maker based in Poznań, Poland.

She illustrates every day life, typical or unusual situations. She likes to juggle between different techniques like screen print, risograph, painting or simple drawing. The combination of artisan production technique, modern graphic design and playful approach became the hallmark of her work.

Kinga Offert es un artista, ilustrador y print maker con sede en Poznań, Polonia.

Ilustra la vida diaria, situaciones típicas o inusuales. Le gusta hacer malabares entre diferentes técnicas como serigrafía, risografía, pintura o dibujo simple. La combinación de técnicas de producción artesanal, diseño gráfico moderno y enfoque lúdico se han convertido en el sello de su trabajo.

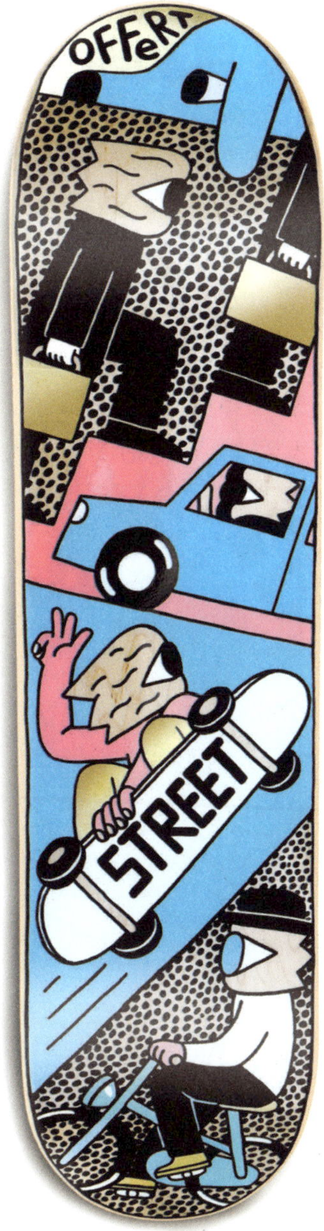

Skateboard CITY // by Kinga Offert

One of a series illustrations related to the city. This board shows the`variety of the street, busy people walking, driving, riding a bike and having fun on skateboard.

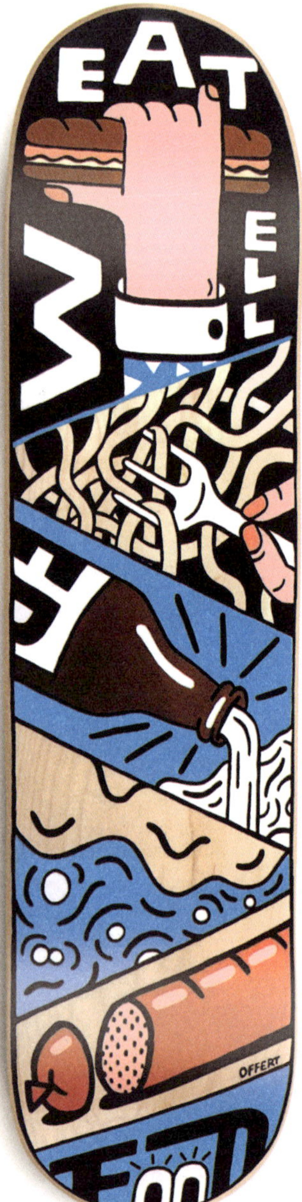

Skateboard EAT // by Kinga Offert

My intention was to “familiarise” people with unique world of good beer and tasty food in a friendly and accessible way.

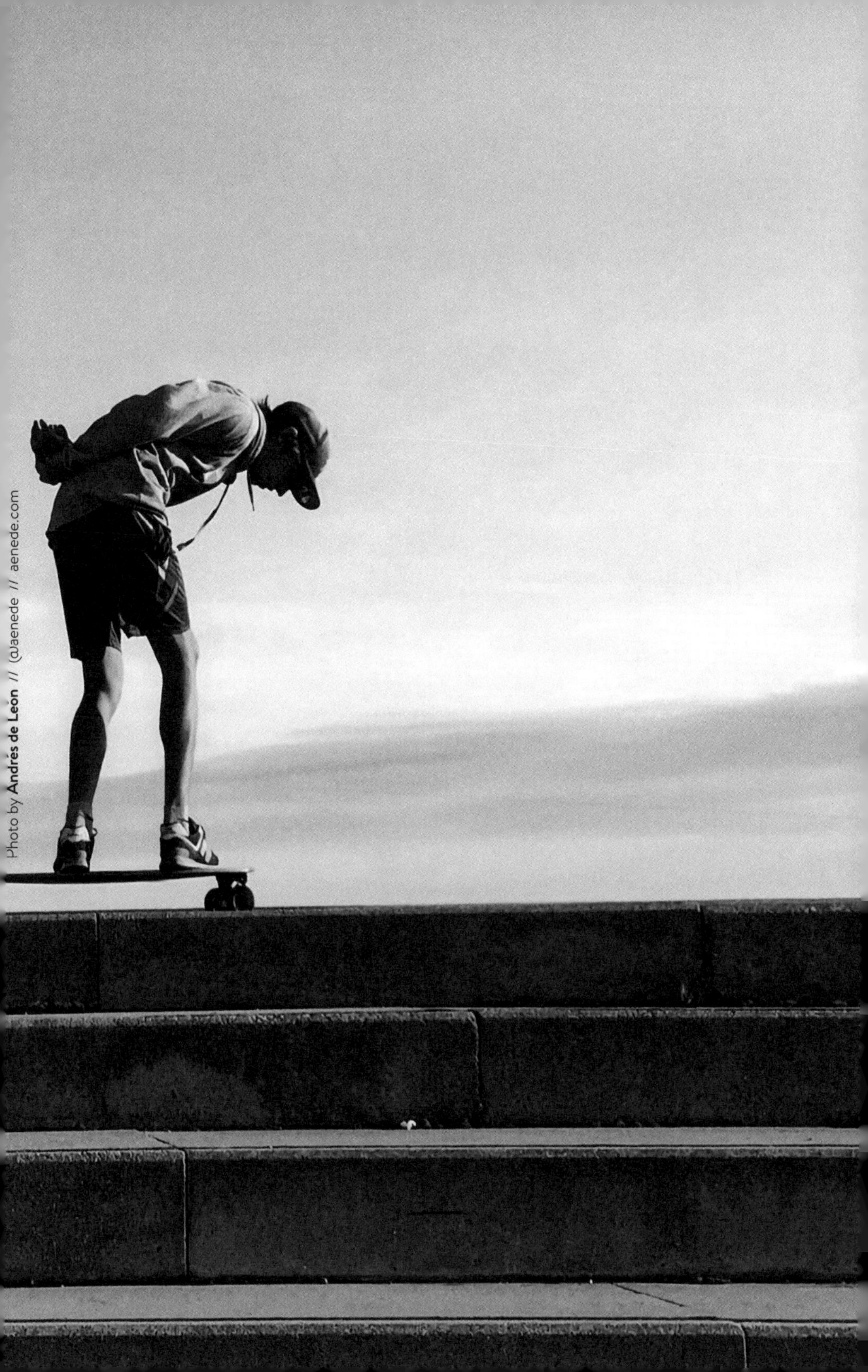

Photo by **Andrés de León** // @aenede // aenede.com

Seth Gale

sethgale.com

Seth Gale is a multi-disciplinary designer based out of Seattle, Washington. Seth's approach to creative work places an emphasis on collaboration, experimentation, and systematic thinking to create distilled, meaningful pieces.

Seth Gale es un diseñador multidisciplinar que reside en Seattle, Washington. El enfoque de Seth hacia el trabajo creativo pone énfasis en la colaboración, la experimentación y el pensamiento sistemático para crear piezas destiladas y significativas.

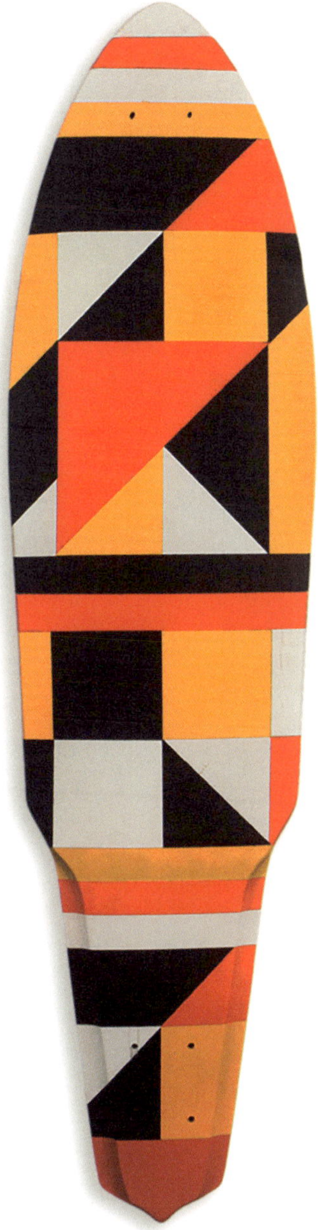

65

Angles // by Seth Gale

Hand-painted board created as part of the Ride On skateboard show.

Cristobal Ojeda Newfren

www.behance.net/newfren

Cristobal is a full time freelance designer and Illustrator from Chile. He studied Bachelor of Design at the University of lakes, Osorno.

Today is dedicated to product design and character design, Cristobal has worked for brands around the world. Some clients are Nike, Billboard, Moods, Redds, Sammontana among others.

Also realizes personal projects that are important for the development of new ideas and graphics.

Cristóbal es un diseñador freelance a tiempo completo e ilustrador de Chile. Licenciado en Diseño en la Universidad de Lagos, Osorno.

Hoy se dedica al diseño de productos y diseño de personajes, ha trabajado para marcas de todo el mundo. Algunos de sus clientes son Nike, Billboard, Moods, Redds, Sammontana entre otros.

También realiza proyectos personales que son importantes para el desarrollo de nuevas ideas y gráficos.

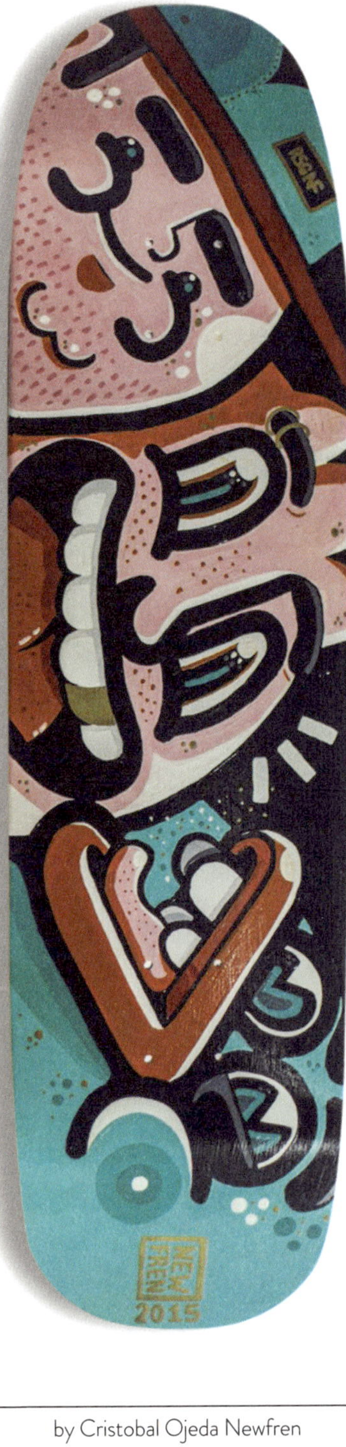

by Cristobal Ojeda Newfren

Boom-art

www.boom-art.com

Boom-art.com is an art gallery dedicated to Skateboarding and Surfing , they publish limited edition and deliver their boards worldwide. They are located in the south of France (Aix en Provence) have a bowl in their garden (holenite pool) , they love Art , Skateboarding and Surfing... and practice as often as possible....	*Boom-art.com es una galería de arte dedicada a Skateboarding y Surfing, que crean ediciones limitadas y entregan sus tablas en todo el mundo.* *Están situados en el sur de Francia (Aix en Provence) tienen un cuenco en su jardín (cuenco de afeitado), les encanta el Arte, el Skateboarding y el Surf...* *Y practicar tantas veces como sea posible...*

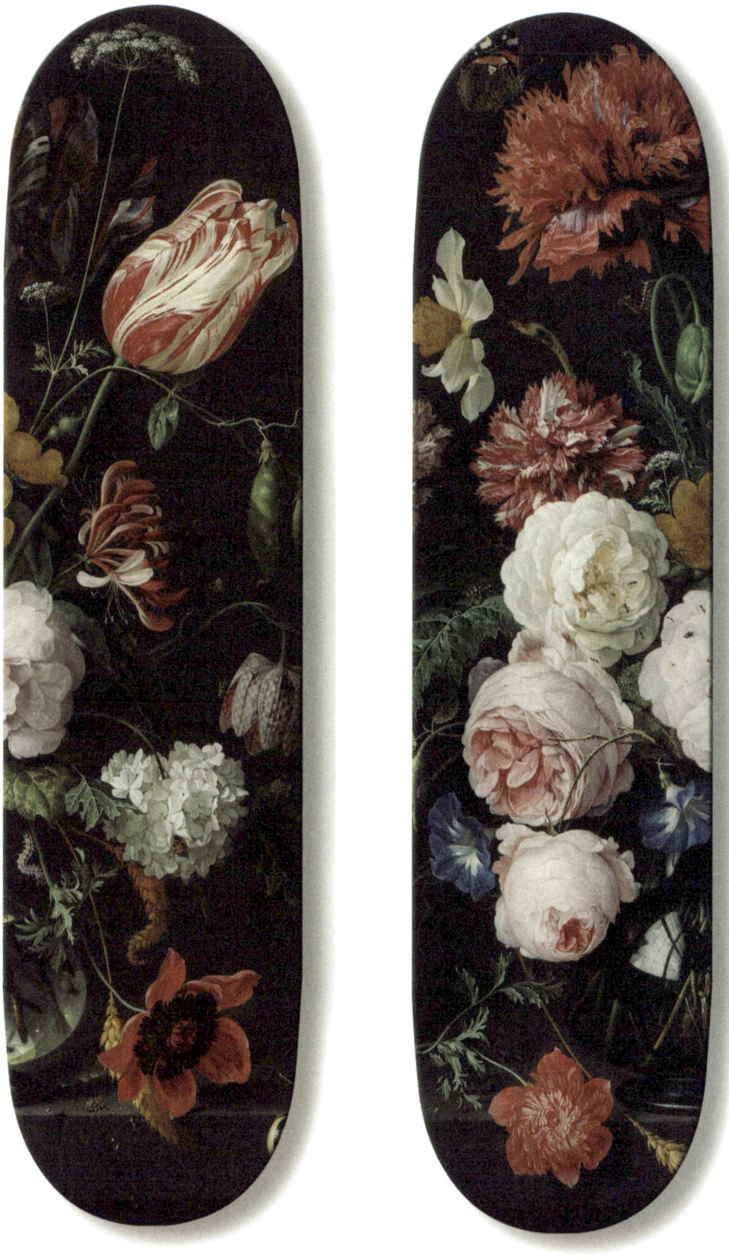

Flowers // by Boom-art

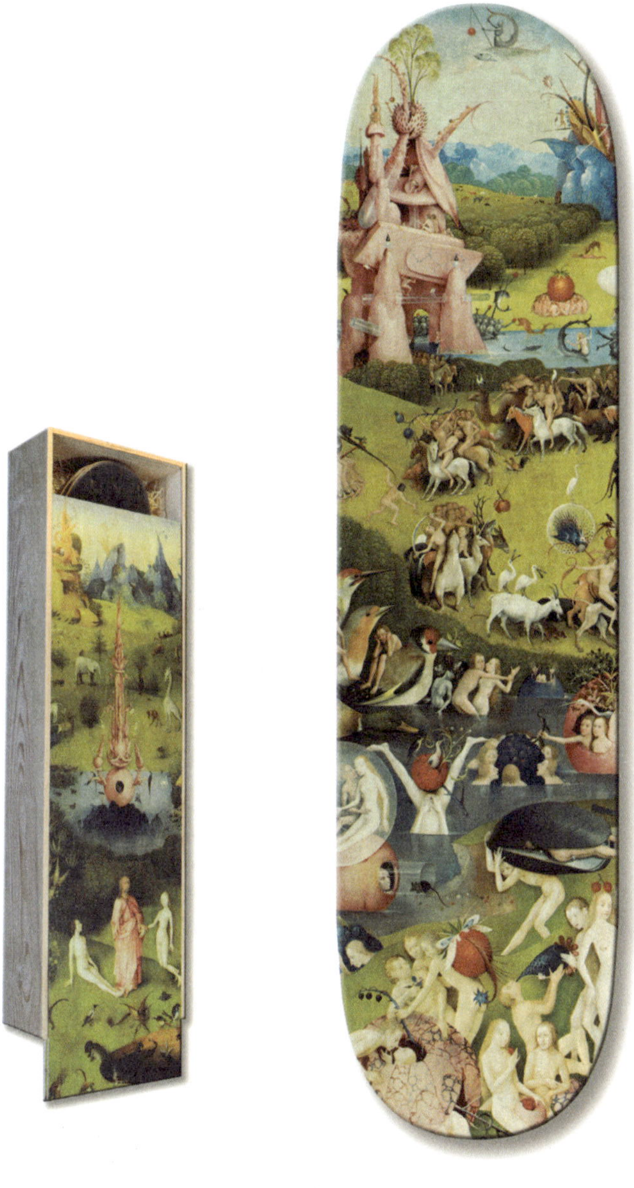

Bosh // by Boom-art

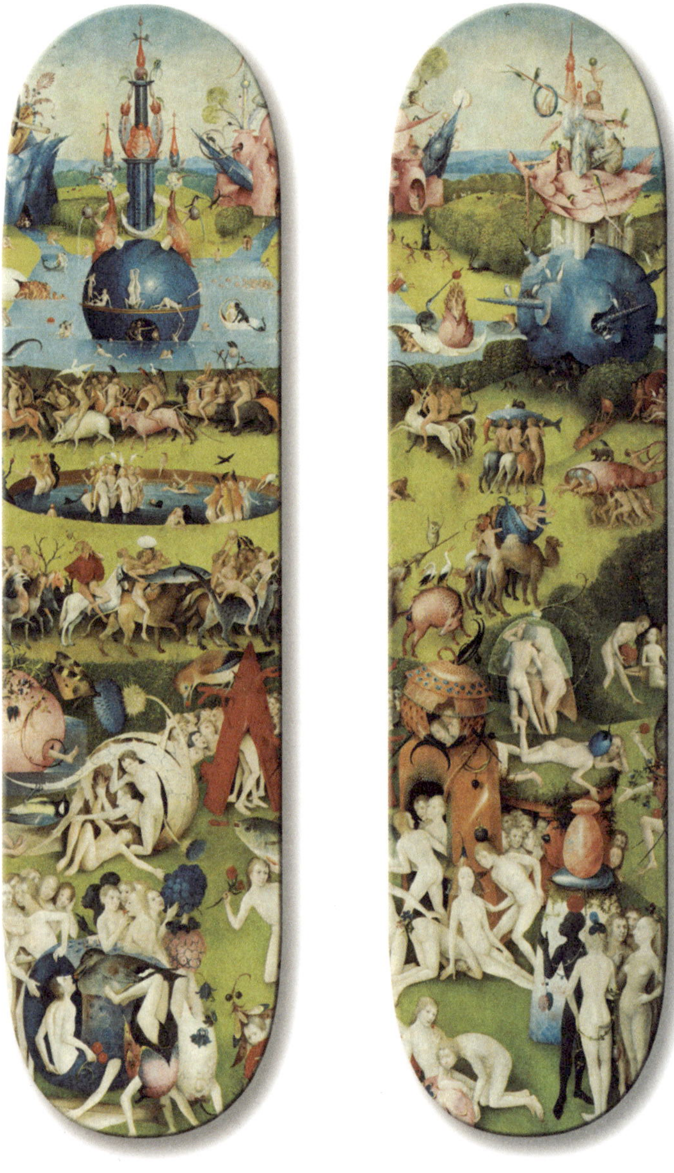

71

Bosh // by Boom-art

72

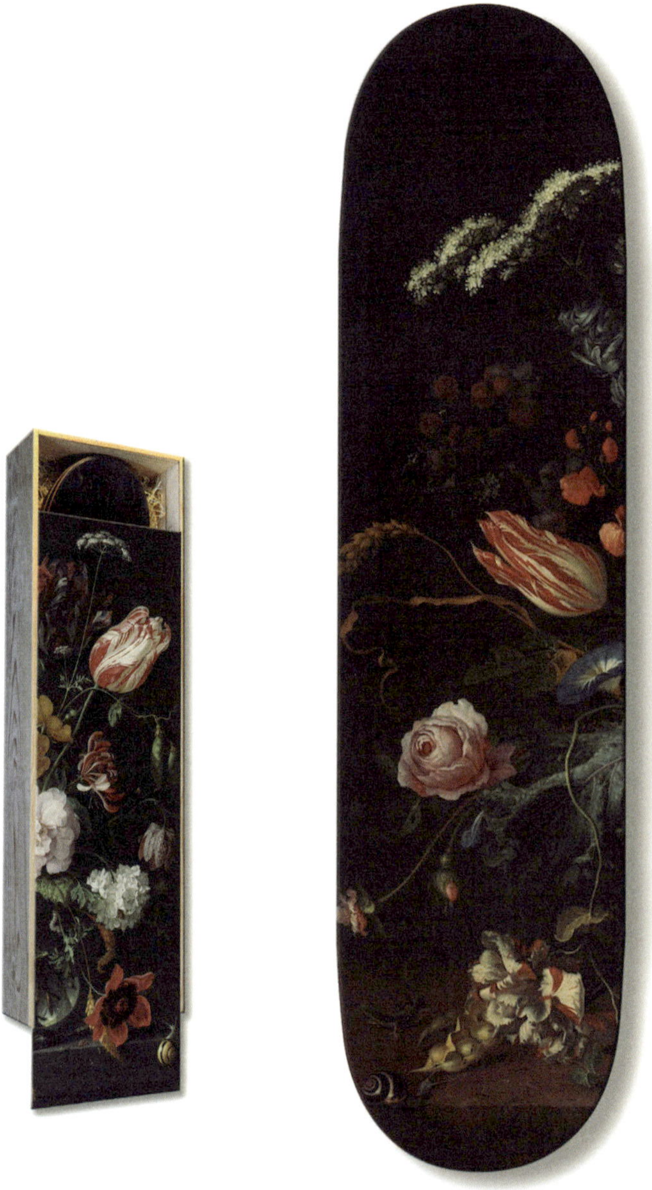

Flowers // by Boom-art

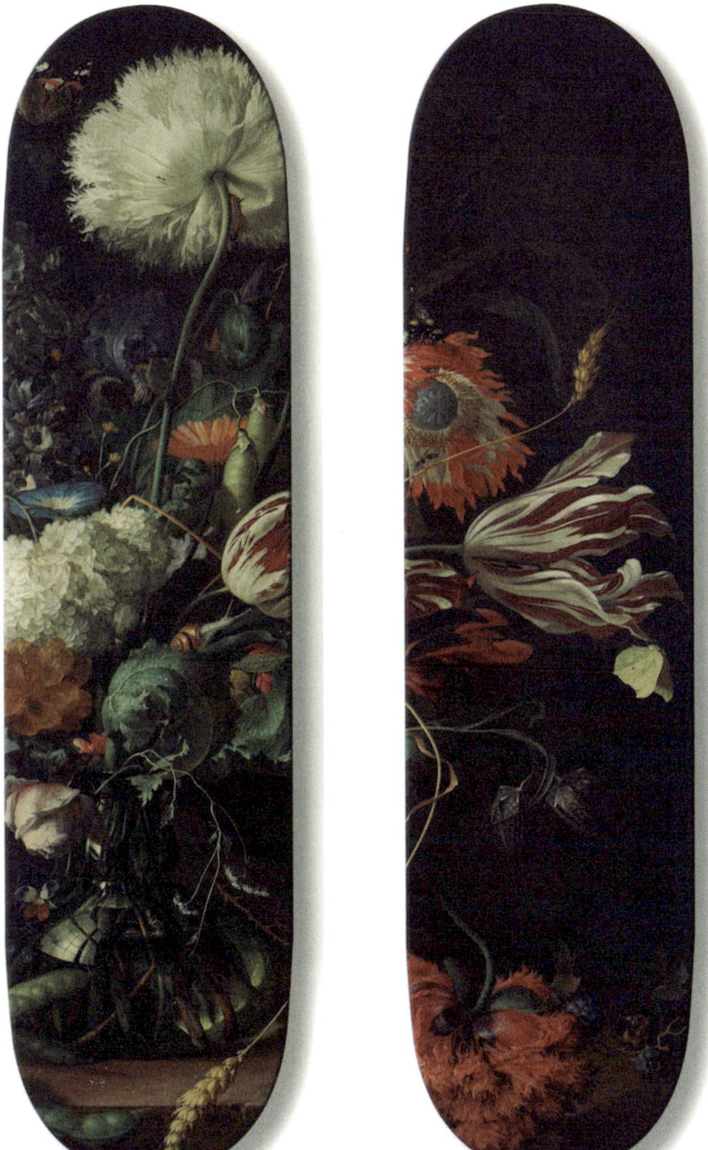

Flowers // by Boom-art

Matacho Descorp

www.matacho.com | instagram: @matachodescorp

Matacho Descorp, an alternative graphic designer with a Masters in publishing design, focuses his work on the personalization of objects ranging from paper toys, skateboards, portable sound systems, clothing and accessories to any format which will allow him to express his graphic ideas in new settings. His design style can be defined as "a controlled chaos of complex elements which combine to create simplicity" or "a controlled chaos of simple elements which combine to create complexity", all depending on the eye of the viewer, who might be able to discern traces of Latin American native roots brought into the present day, and a display of Latin power for the delight of lovers of graphic art.

Matacho Descorp, diseñador gráfico alternativo con un máster en diseño editorial, concentra su trabajo en la personalización de objetos que van desde papertoys, skateboards, sistemas de audio portable, ropa, accesorios y cualquier soporte que permita llevar su propuesta gráfica a nuevos escenarios, su estilo de diseño se puede definir como un "caos controlado de elementos complejos que funcionan en simplicidad", o un "caos controlado de elementos simples que funcionan en complejidad", todo depende de la mirada del espectador que pueda notar en estos trazos las raíces latinoamericanas indígenas llevadas a la actualidad, una nueva propuesta llena de poder latino para el deleite de los amantes de la gráfica.

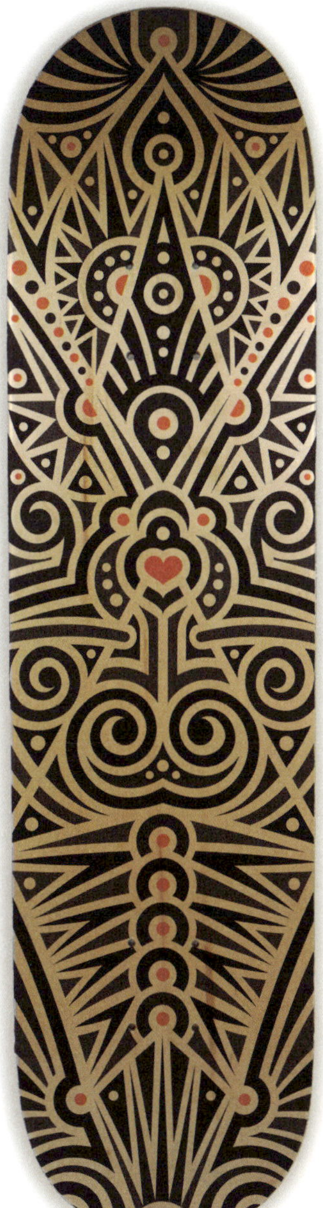

Personal Artwork // by Matacho Descorp

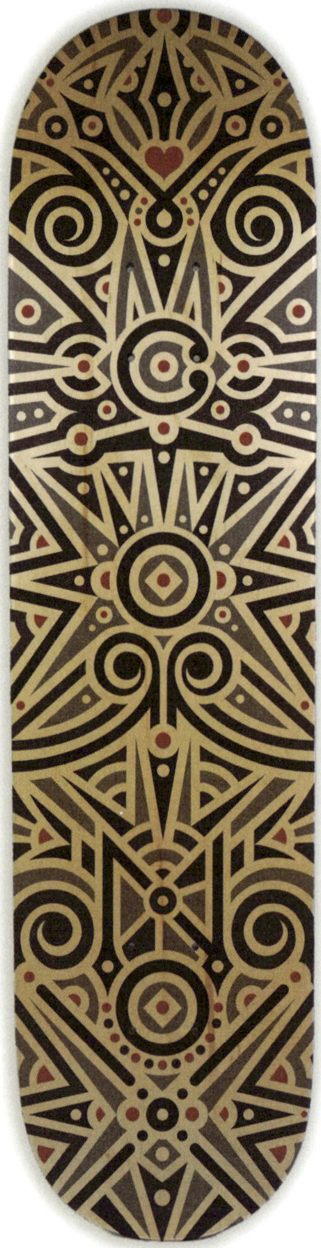

Personal Artwork // by Matacho Descorp

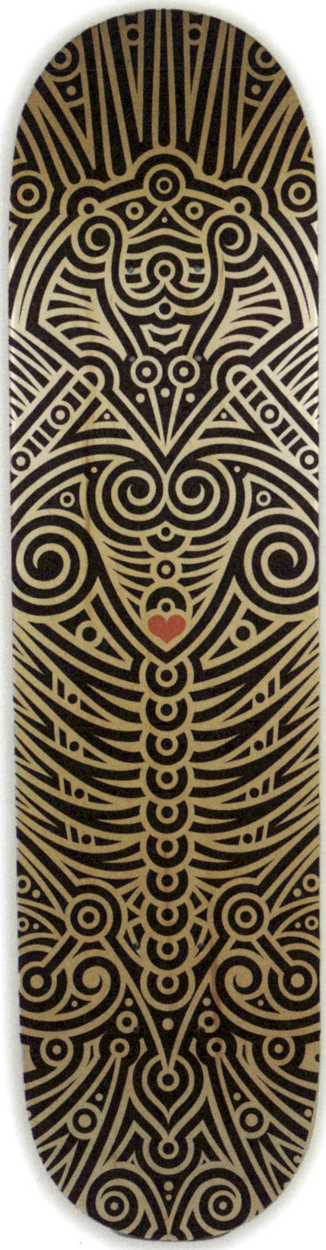

Shove it project // by Matacho Descorp

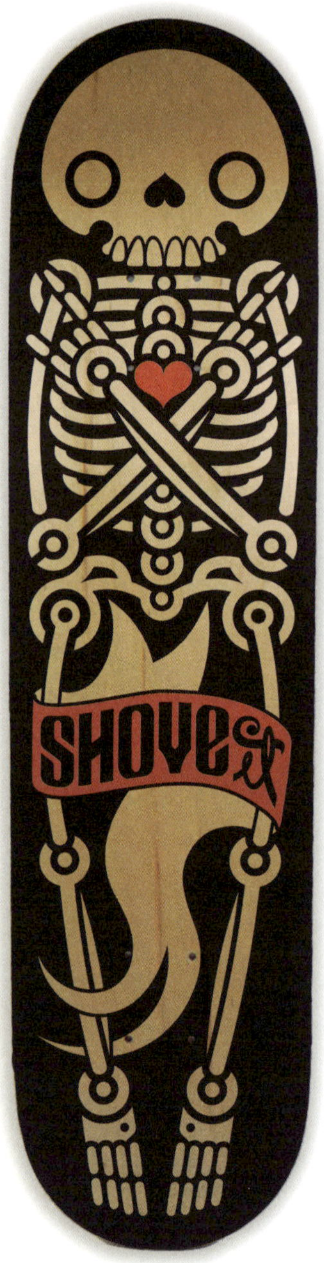

Shove it project // by Matacho Descorp

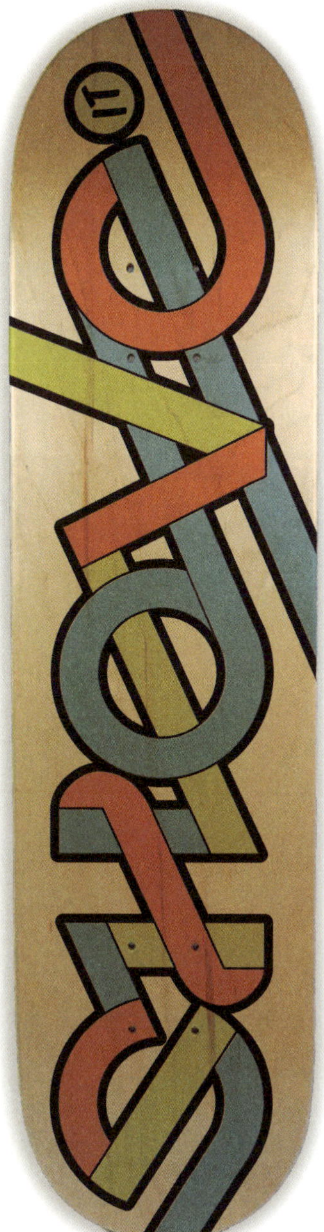

Shove it project // by Matacho Descorp

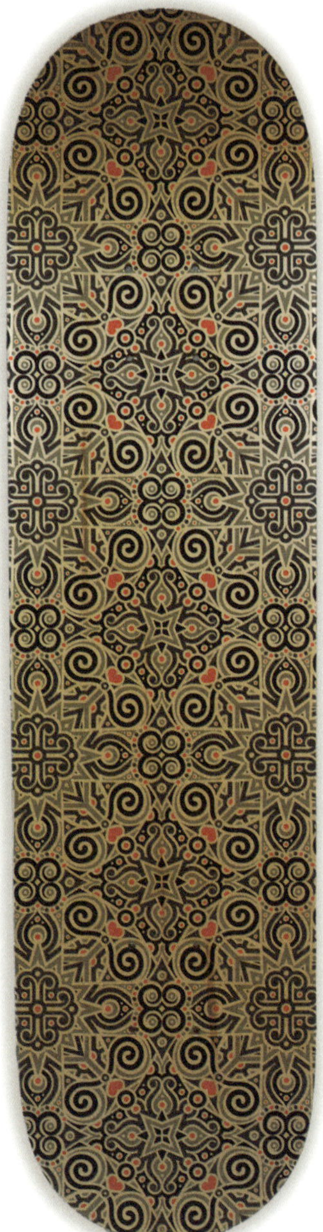

Personal Artwork // by Matacho Descorp

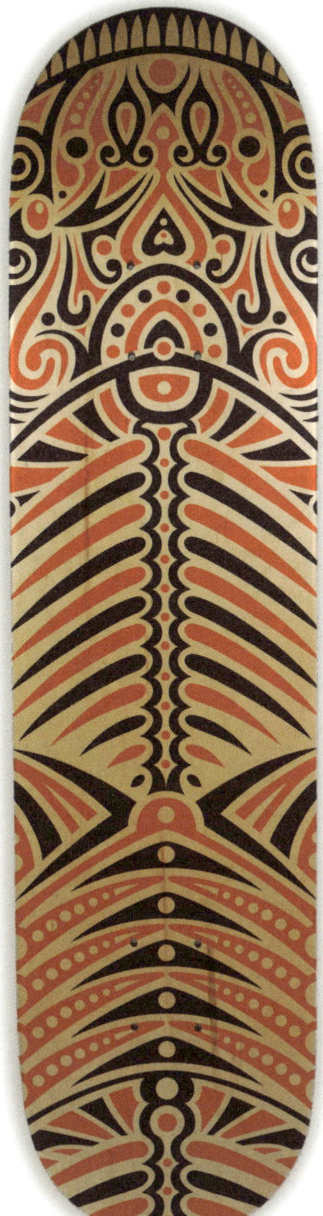

81

Personal Artwork // by Matacho Descorp

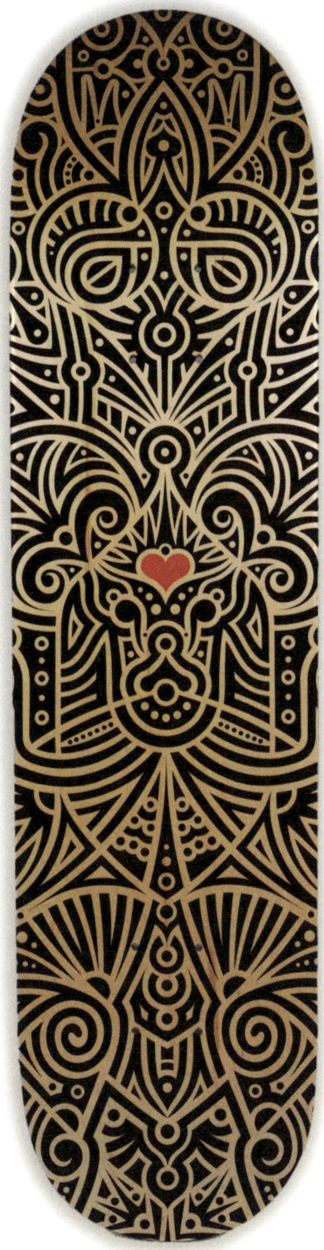

Posca contest // by Matacho Descorp // for Posca

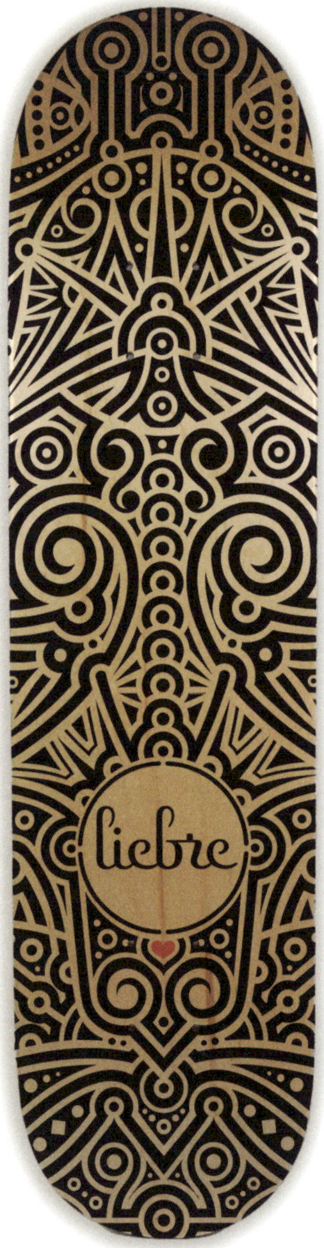

by Matacho Descorp // for Liebre Boards

Joan Tarragó

www.joantarrago.com	instagram: @joantarrago

Joan Tarragó is a Barcelona based Illustrator. His career started 12 years ago when he moved to Athens for a school internship. Since this time he became modern nomad of everyday life, always on the move between Berlin, Paris, Biarritz, NY, Miami, Thailand, Bulgaria, Gambia, etc. He is in an interdisciplinary journey between illustration and street art, two- and three-dimensionality. He believes illustration is no longer bound by the flat format, but very often inspects and develops space. With his projects he tries to build bridges between art and design, where illustration, painting, street & communication all play an important role.

Joan Tarragó es un ilustrador residente en Barcelona. Su carrera comenzó hace 12 años al mudarse a Atenas a vivir en un internado. A partir de ese momento se volvió un nómada moderno, cada día de un sitio a otro, viajando entre Barcelona, Berlín, París, Biarritz, Nueva York, Richmond, Miami, Tailandia, Bulgaria, Gambia, Copenhagen, etc. Su estilo es un viaje interdisciplinario entre la ilustración y el arte callejero, en dos o tres dimensiones. Cree que la ilustración está destinada a abandonar parcialmente el formato plano y por esa razón inspecciona y desarrolla el espacio. Con sus proyectos intenta crear puentes entre el arte y el diseño, en donde la ilustración, la pintura, la calle y la comunicación juegan un importante rol.

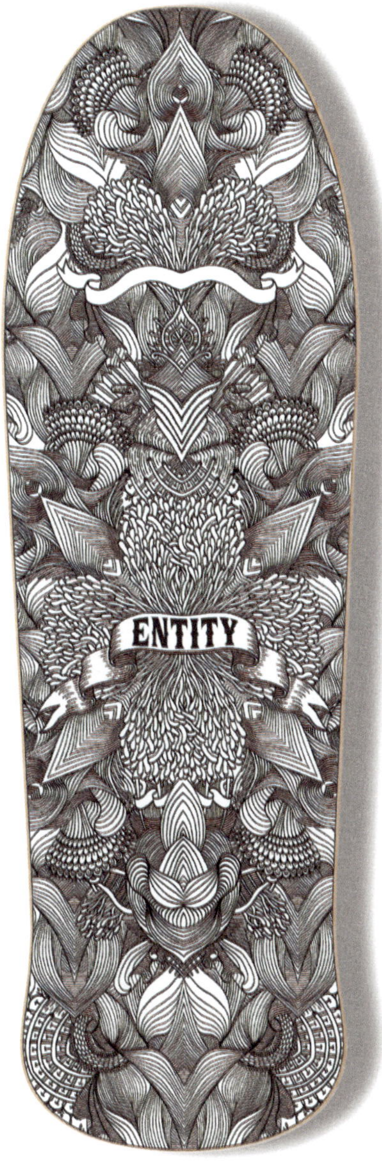

Entity Skate // by Joan Tarragó // for Entity Life (Clothing Company)

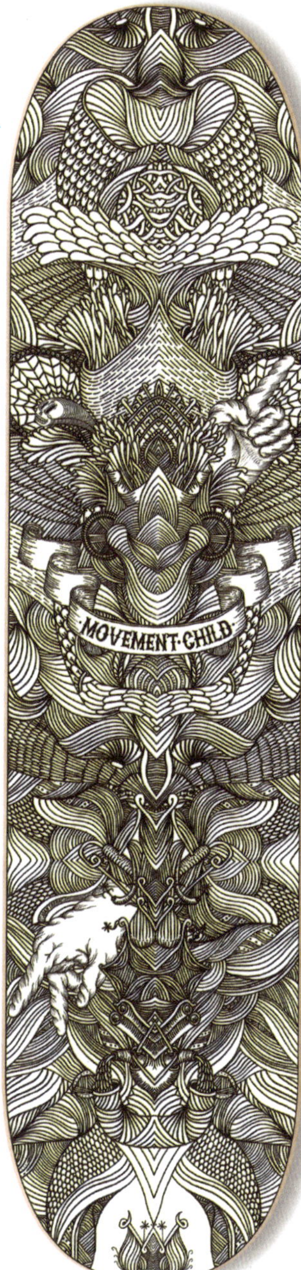

Movement Child Skateboard // by Joan Tarragó

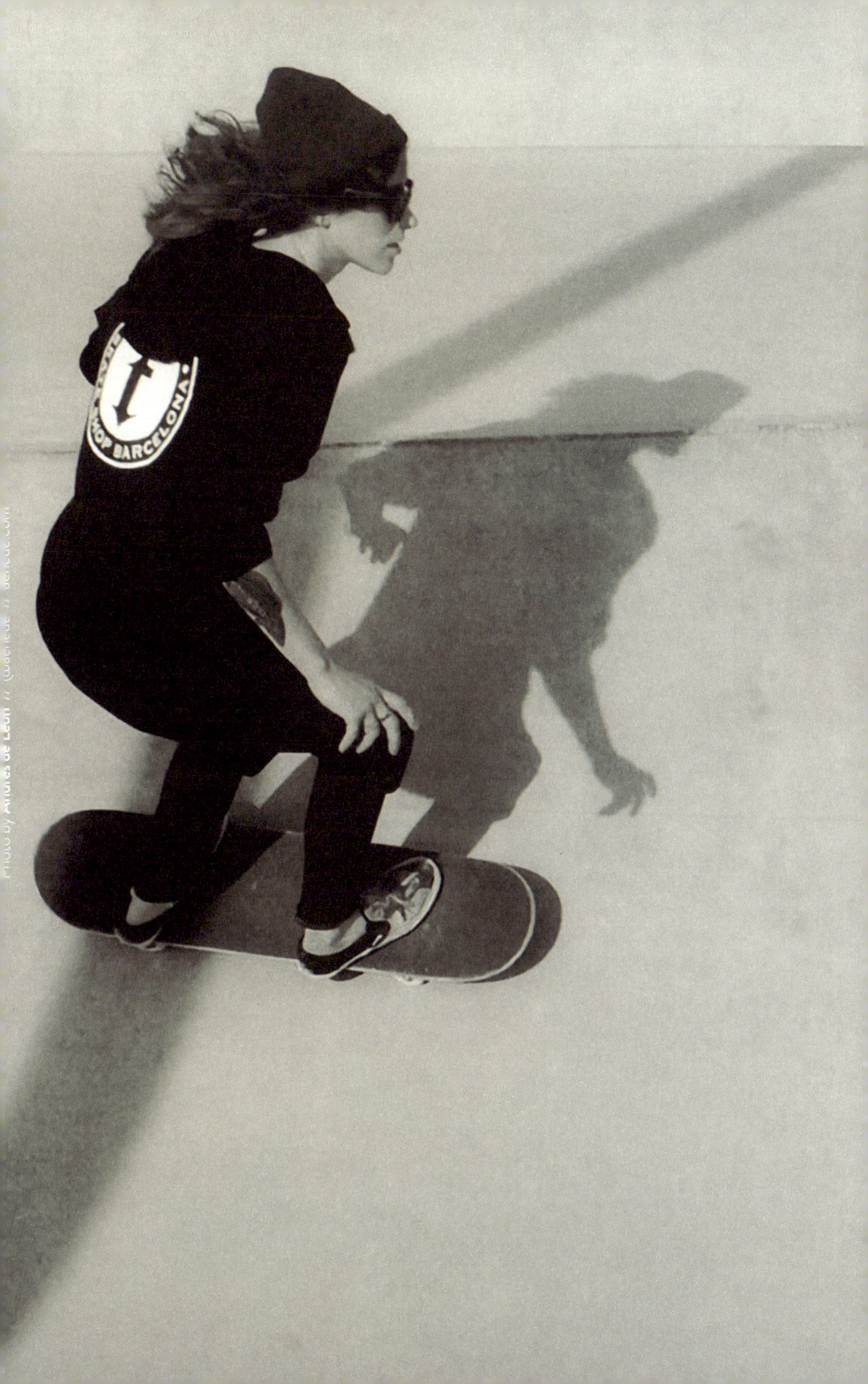

Photo by Andres de Leon

Isaac Malakkai

malakkai.es

Isaac Malakkai, was raised in Barcelona but born in Almería. He always had a pencil in hand but never realized it was what he wanted to dedicate himself to until he was studying telecommunications. He had a lonstanding interest in graffiti, which aroused his passion for drawing; travelling and getting to meet other artists from around the globe. His work can be seen on walls from Almería to Gerona, Lyon, Belgrade, Ciudad de Juarez, Tunisia, and Nuremberg and beyond.

Lover of the Bic biro, the feminine form, whales, cool shades of colour, and with a fixation with the internal problems that are so difficult to externalize, all combined with irony and a surreal sense of humour.

Isaac Malakkai, fue gestado en Barcelona pero nacido en Almería. Siempre tuvo el lápiz en la mano pero no se dio cuenta de qué era lo que realmente quería hasta que se vio estudiando telecomunicaciones. Conoció el graffiti, hecho que avivó su pasión por dibujar; viajar y conocer otros artistas por diferentes partes del planeta. Se pueden encontrar obras suyas en muros perdidos por Almería o Girona, desde Lyon, hasta Belgrado, Ciudad de Juarez, Túnez, Nuremberg.

Amante del boli Bic, la figura femenina, los cetáceos y las gamas de color desaturadas, con fijación por los problemas del interior que tanto cuesta exteriorizar, todo mezclado con ironía y un surrealista sentido del humor.

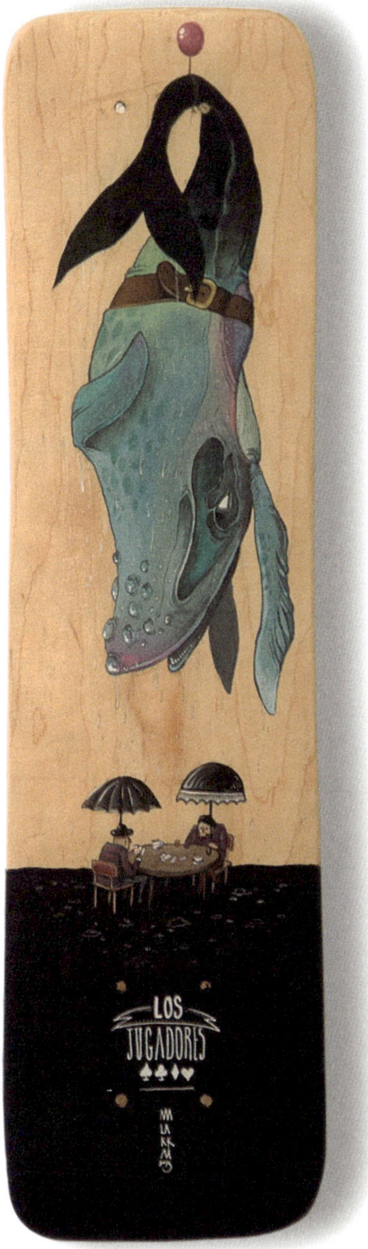

89

Los jugadores // by Isaac Malakkai

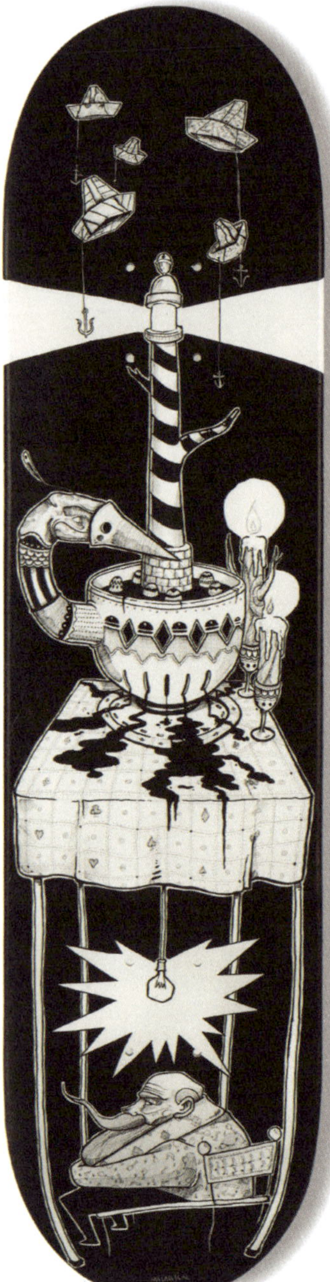

Malakatablaka // by Isaac Malakkai

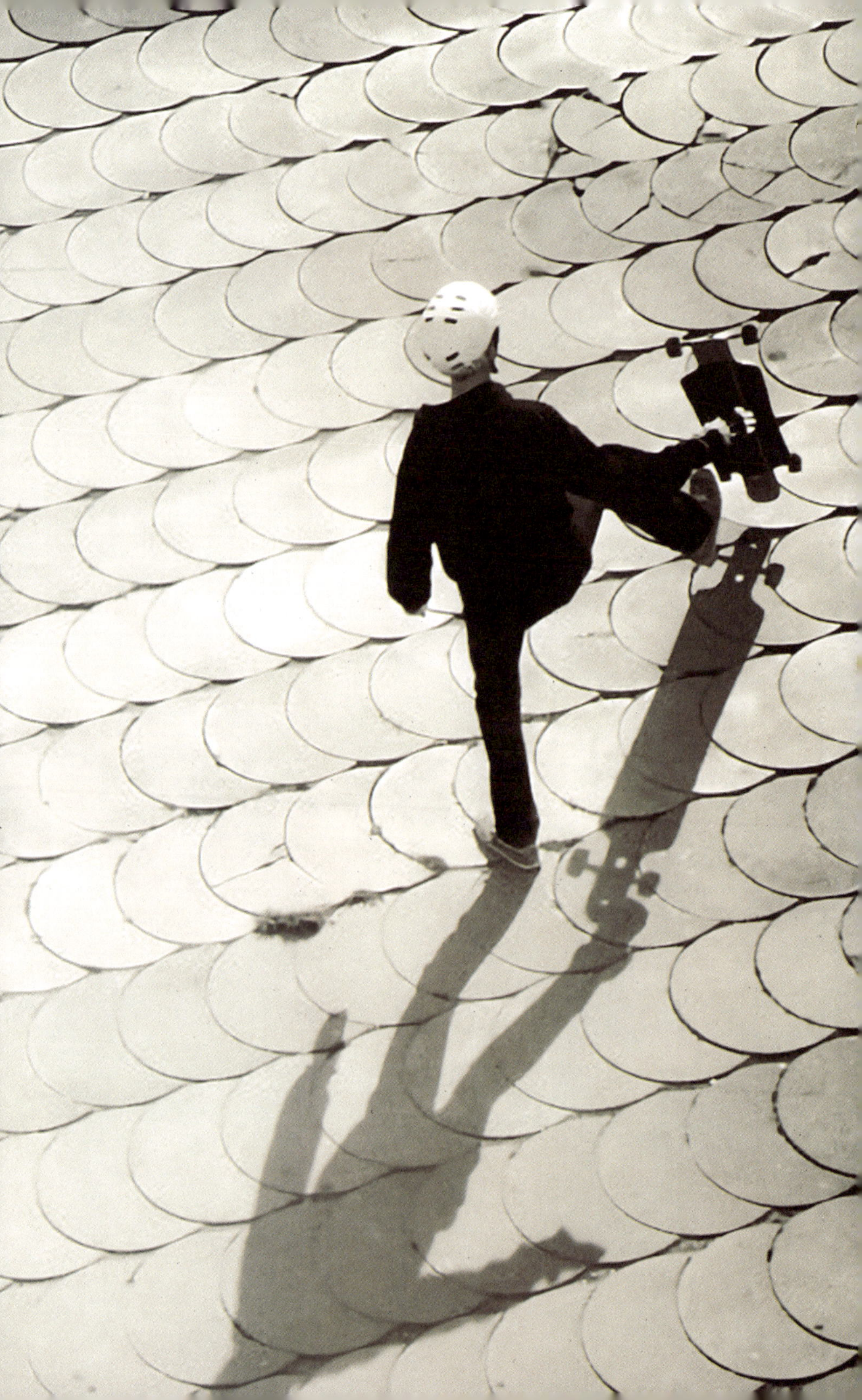

Photo by Andrés de León

Davide Pagliardini

www.davidepagliardini.com	instagram: @davidepagliardini
Davide Pagliardini is a motion and graphic designer. His work is divided between teaching, assignments and his co-founded studio Uovo Lab. Oh, and he loves lettering.	*Davide Pagliardini es un diseñador gráfico y de movimiento. Su trabajo se divide entre la enseñanza, las asignaciones y su co-fundado estudio Uovo Lab. Ah, y le encanta el lettering.*

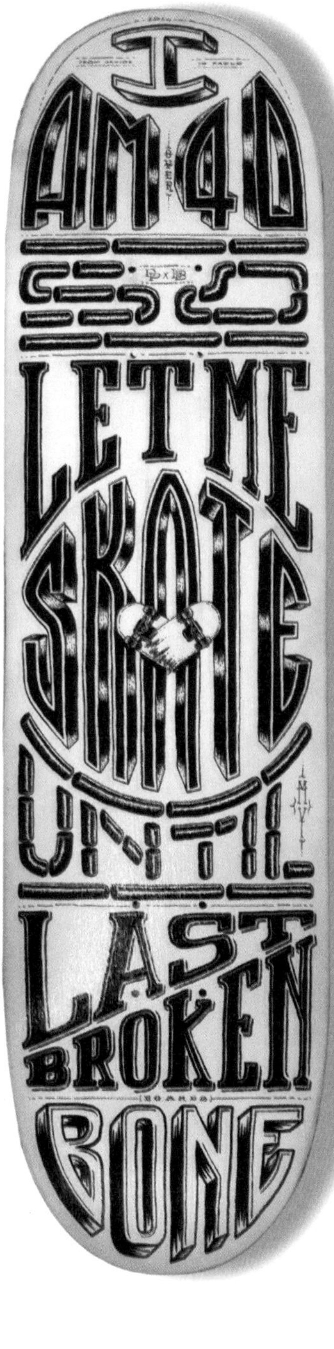

Let me skate // by Davide Pagliardini

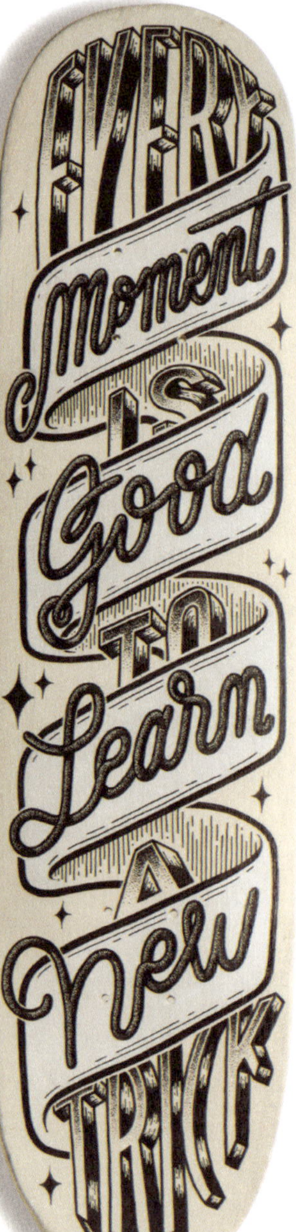

Lear a new trick // by Davide Pagliardini

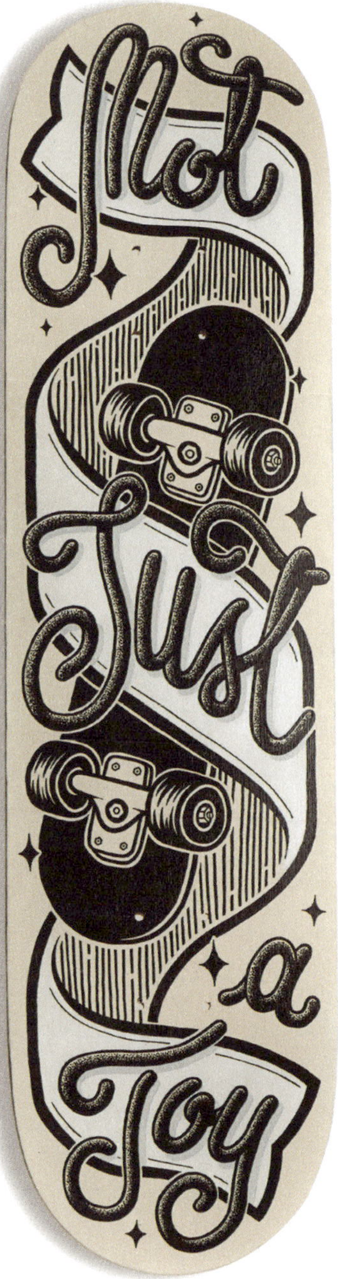

Not just a toy // by Davide Pagliardini

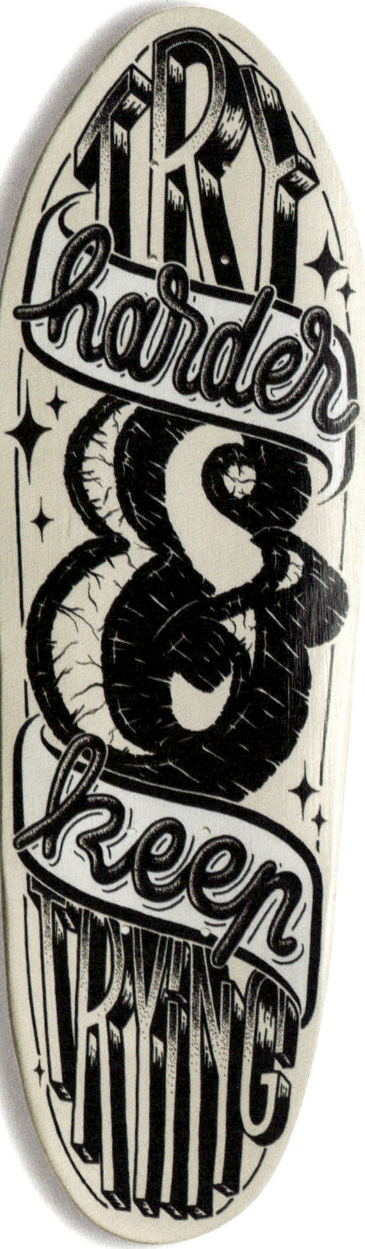

Try harder & keep trying // by Davide Pagliardini

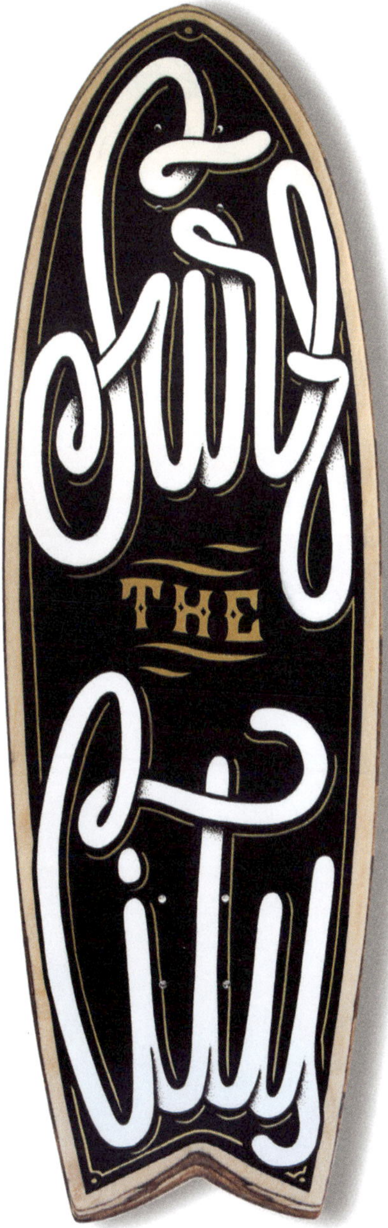

97

Surf the city // by Davide Pagliardini

Bart Aalbers

www.bartaalbers.com

Bart Aalbers is an illustrator from Rotterdam, the Netherlands, with a graphically clean style filled with weird characters, vivid contrasting colours, custom lettering, silly jokes and mid-century nostalgia.

Bart started in his local punk rock scene creating merchandise for bands and now works for a big variety of clients including Samsung, Booking.com and McDonalds.

Bart Aalbers es un ilustrador de Rotterdam, Países Bajos, con un estilo gráficamente limpio lleno de personajes extraños, contrastes de vivos colores, lettering, chistes tontos y nostalgia de mediados de siglo.

Bart se inició en su escena punk rock local creando diseños para las bandas y ahora trabaja para una gran variedad de clientes entre los que se encuentran Samsung, Booking.com y McDonalds.

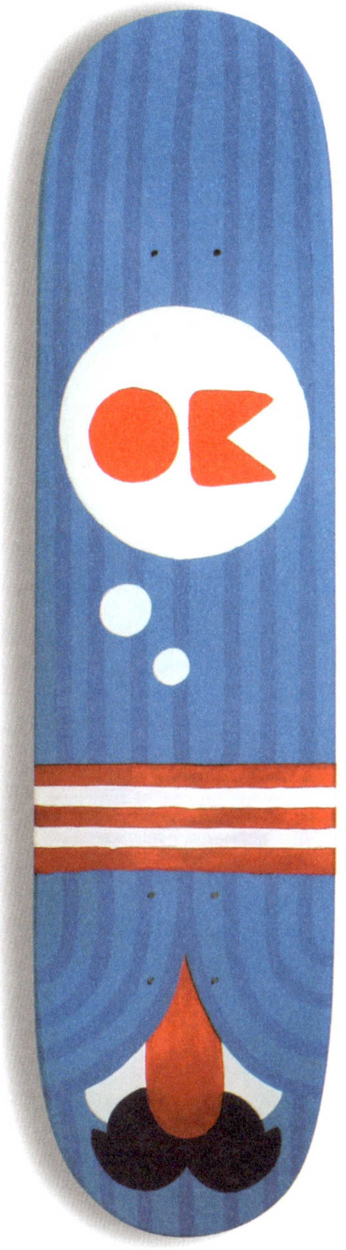

OK/GO Skateboards // by Bart Aalbers

Set of handpainted decks. Acrylics on wood.

100

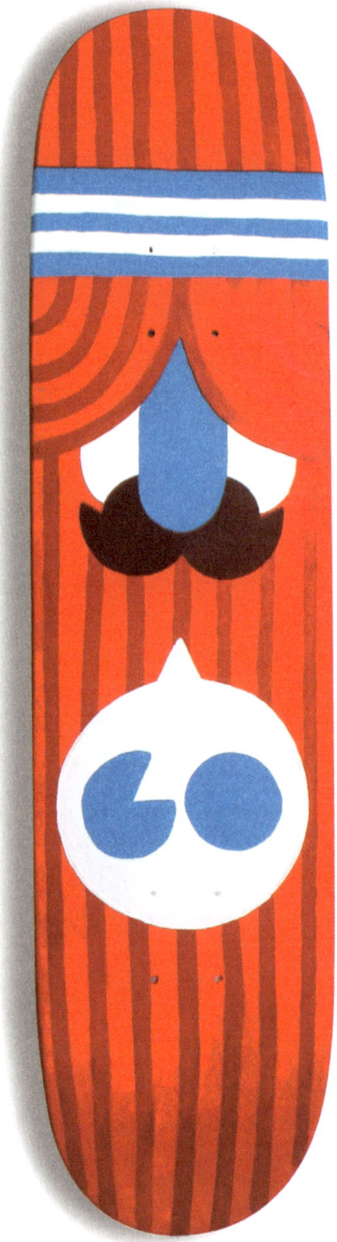

OK/GO Skateboards // by Bart Aalbers

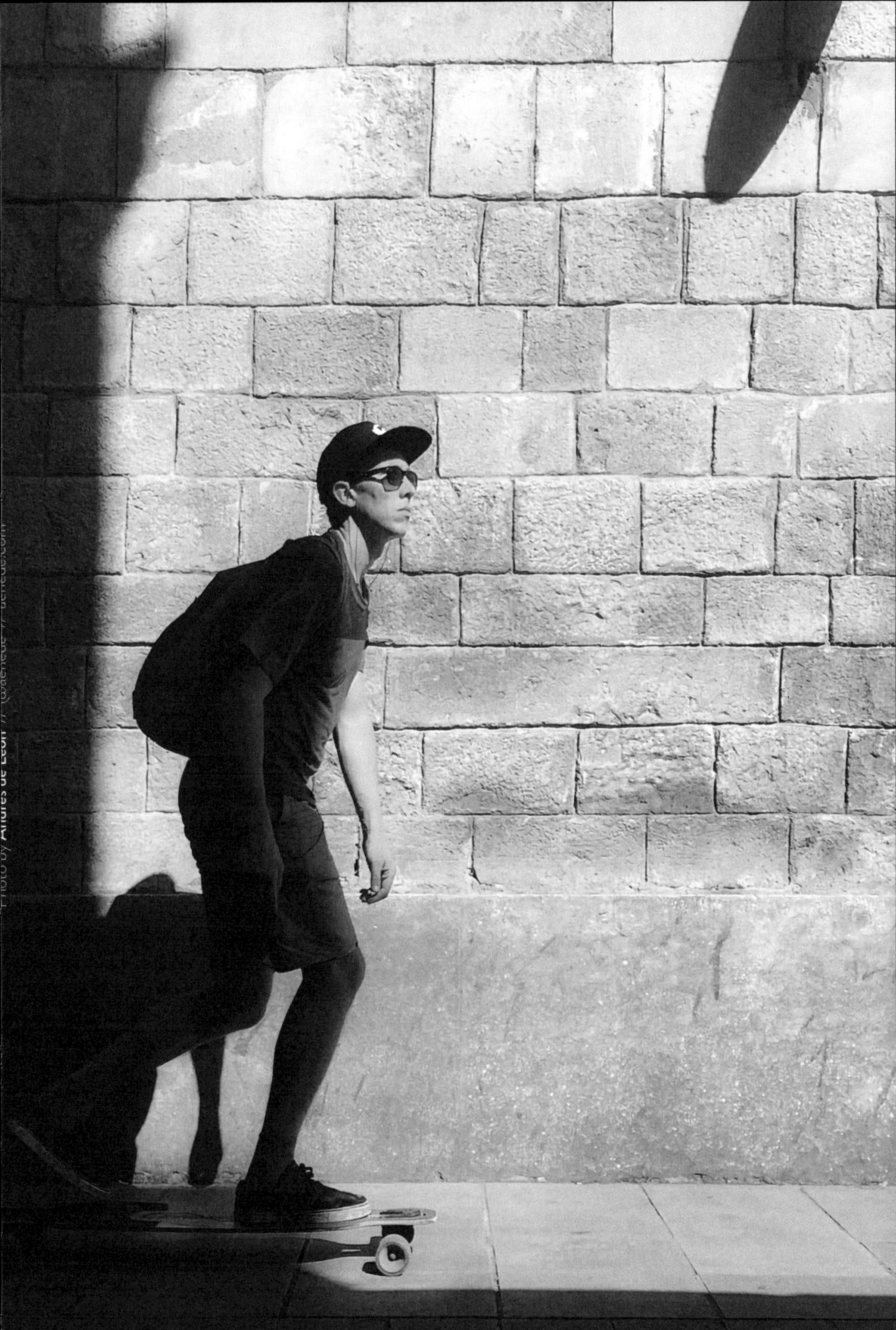
Photo by Andrés de León // @aenede // aenede.com

Caleigh Illerbrun

www.caleigh-ill.com

Caleigh Illerbrun is a Canadian artist/ illustrator currently living in the United Kingdom. Being surrounded by a completely different landscape in the UK, she started to notice more and more imagery from her home country appearing in her work, realising how much the place where you grow up can be so ingrained in your soul. She loves to explore the different relationships between creatures without the distraction of human presence, in order to explore more universal qualities through her work.

Caleigh Illerbrun es un artista / ilustrador canadiense que actualmente vive en el Reino Unido. Estando rodeada por un paisaje completamente diferente en el Reino Unido, comenzó a incluir más y más imágenes de su país de origen en su trabajo, dándose cuenta de cómo puede estar tan arraigada su alma al lugar donde creces. Le encanta explorar las diferentes relaciones entre las criaturas sin la distracción de la presencia humana, con el fin de mostrar las cualidades más universales a través de su trabajo.

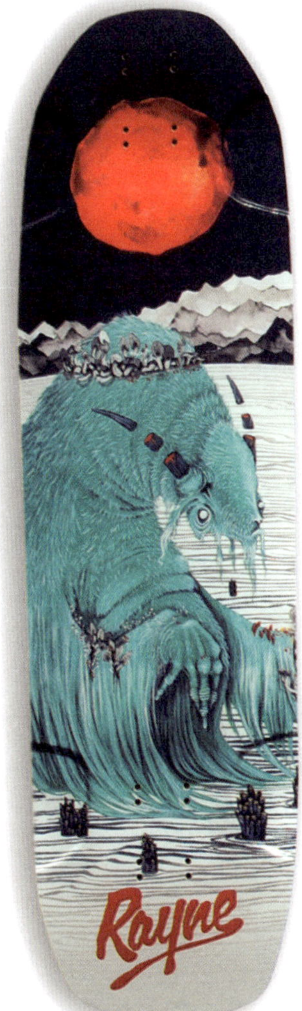

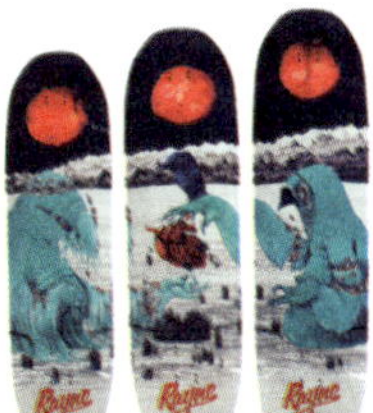

Blood Moon // by Caleigh Illerbrun // for Rayne

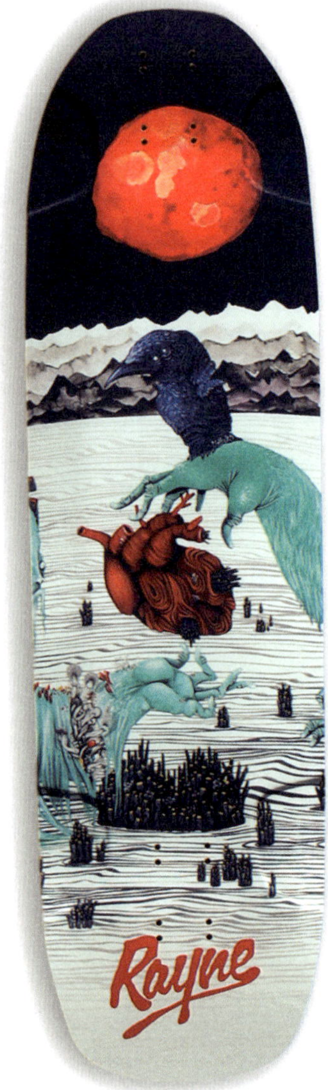

Blood Moon // by Caleigh Illerbrun // for Rayne

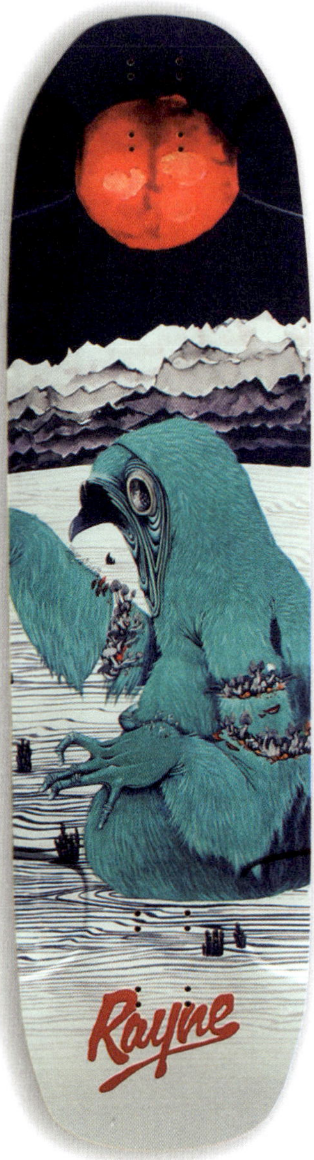

Blood Moon // by Caleigh Illerbrun // for Rayne

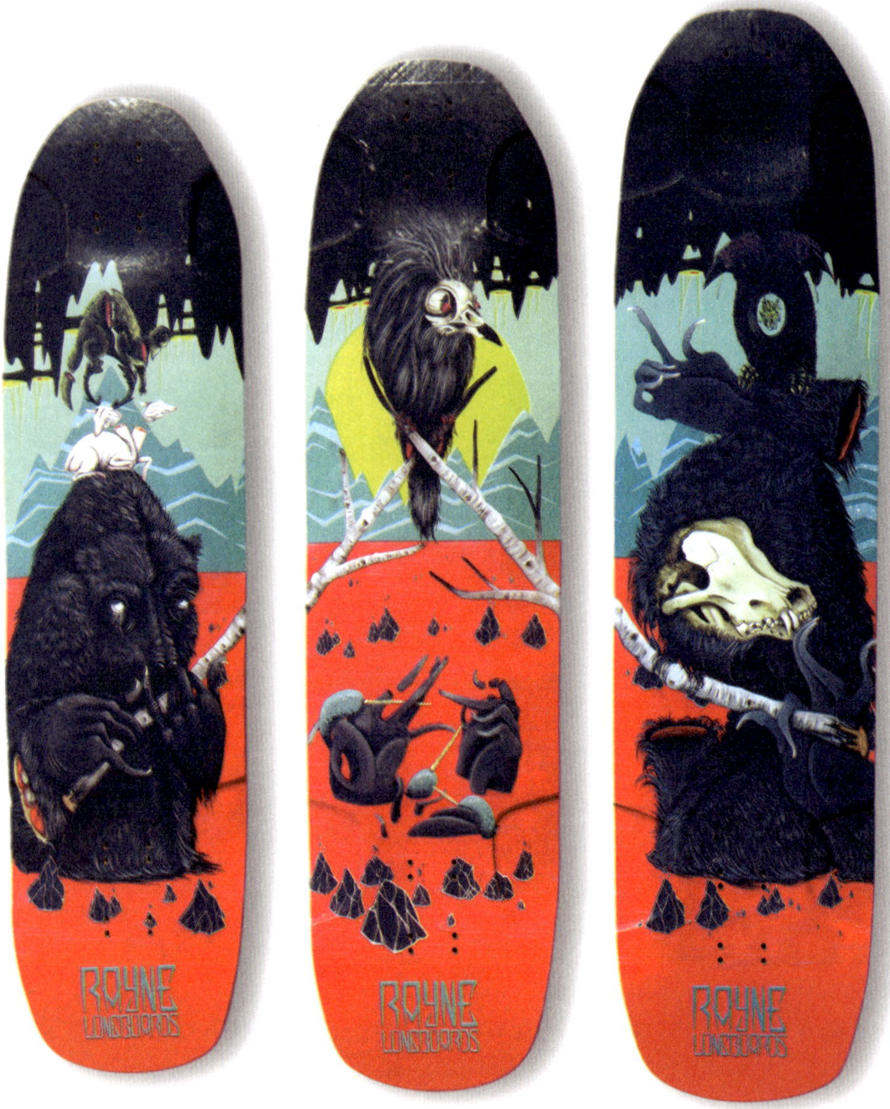

Darkside // by Caleigh Illerbrun // for Rayne

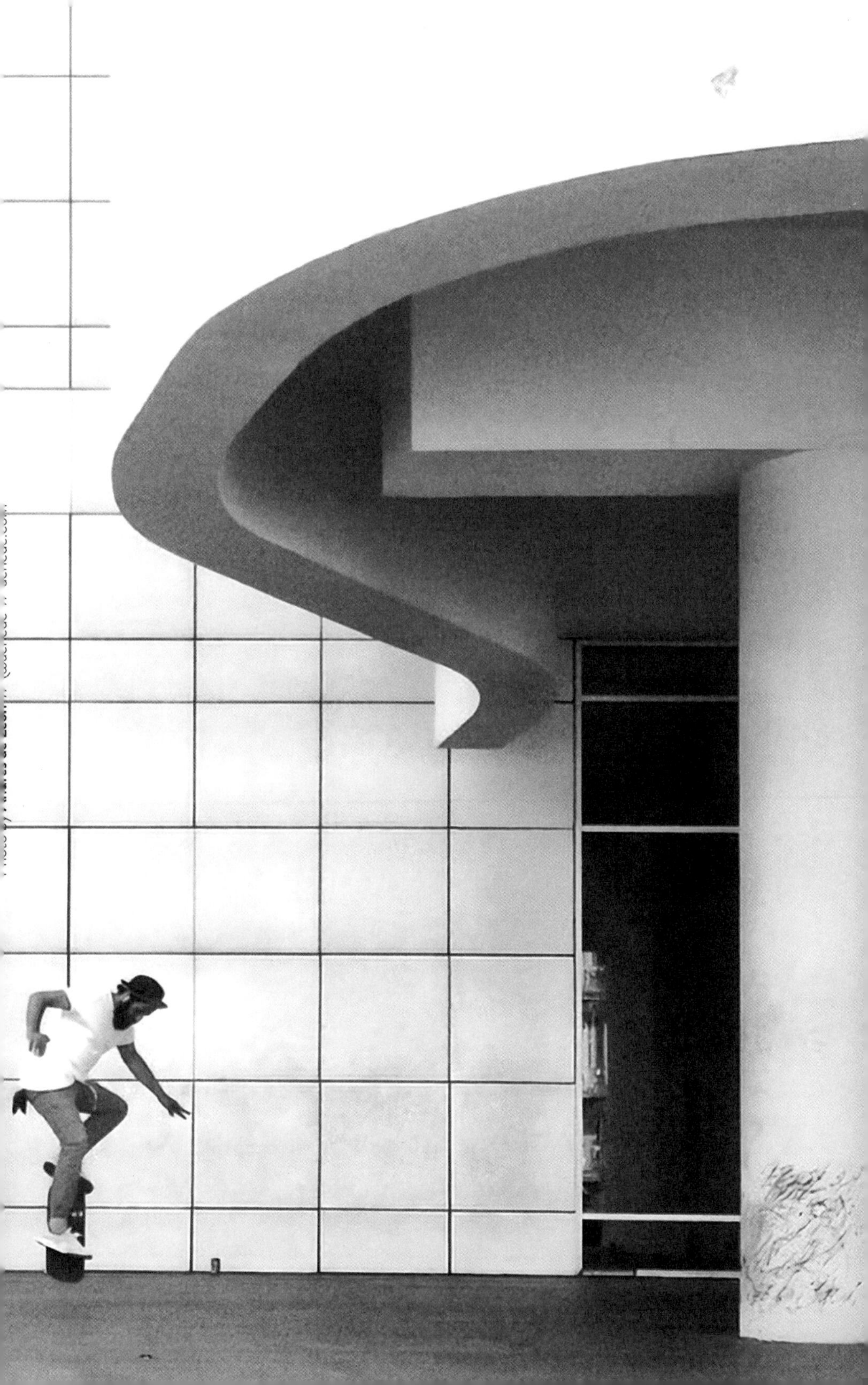

Anton Repponen

www.repponen.com | blog.repponen.com

Anton Repponen is a designer and photographer based in Brooklyn, New York. His main focus is designing large scale interactive projects, design languages and tools that lots of people will use on a daily basis. As a designer he doesn't limit himself with interaction projects only and experiments a lot with physical objects and graphic design.

Anton Repponen es un diseñador y fotógrafo con sede en Brooklyn, Nueva York. Su enfoque principal es el diseño de proyectos interactivos a gran escala, lenguajes de diseño y herramientas que mucha gente usará diariamente. Como diseñador no se limita solo a proyectos de interacción, sino que experimenta mucho con objetos físicos y de diseño gráfico.

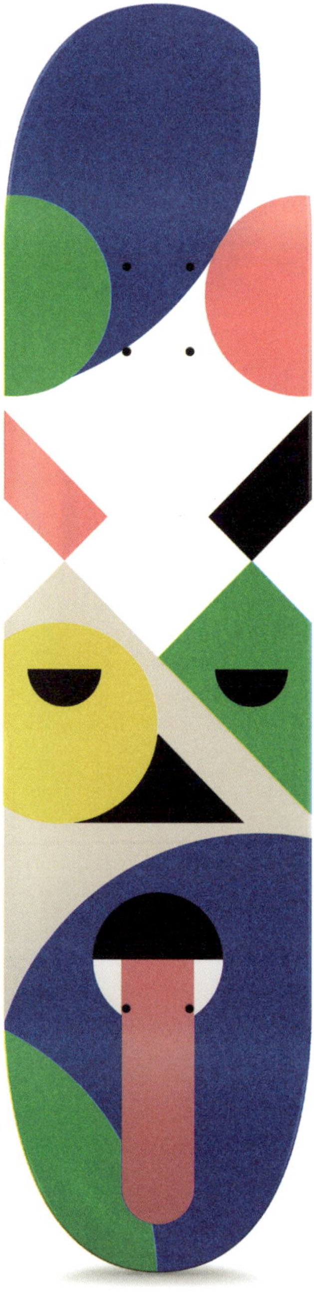

Masks // by Anton Repponen

The shape of a skateboard is somewhat reminds you of various masks that you can see in history museums. Applying minimalistic graphic shapes that resemble different faces makes it look like a mask that you can hang on a wall or attach trucks and go skateboarding with style.

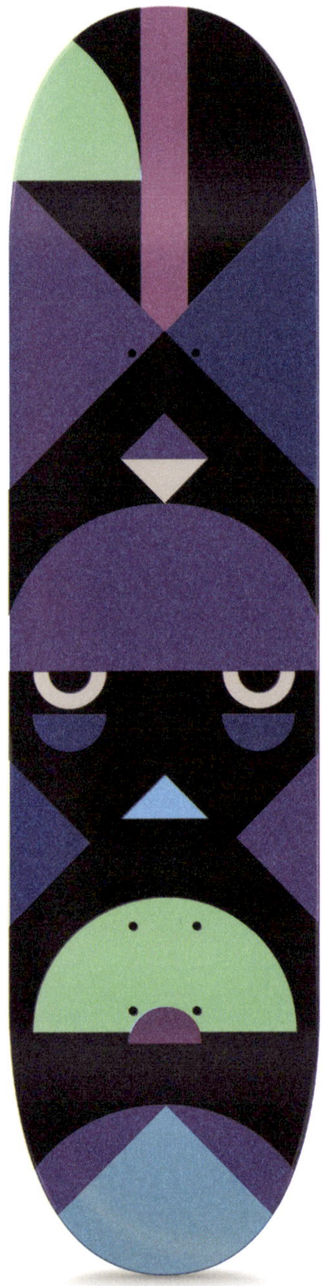

Masks // by Anton Repponen

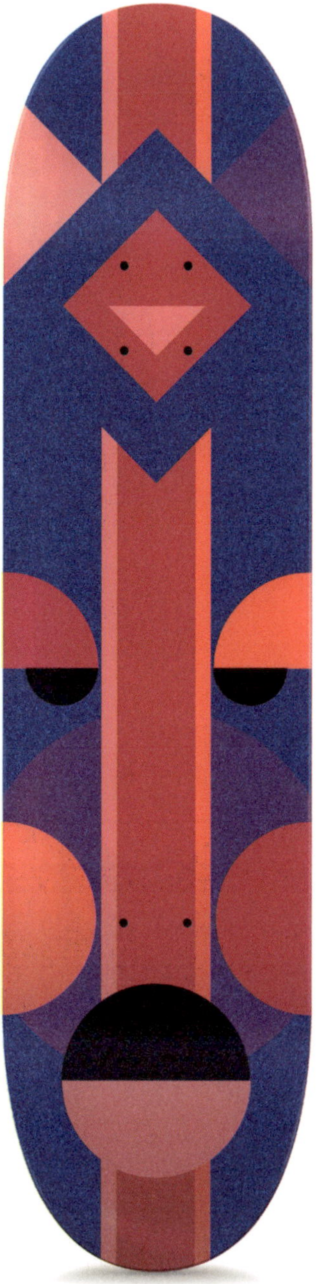

Masks // by Anton Repponen

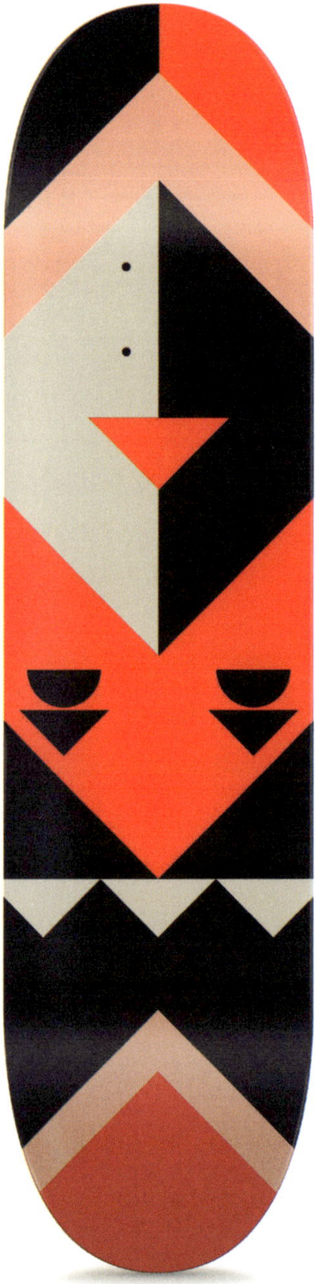

Masks // by Anton Repponen

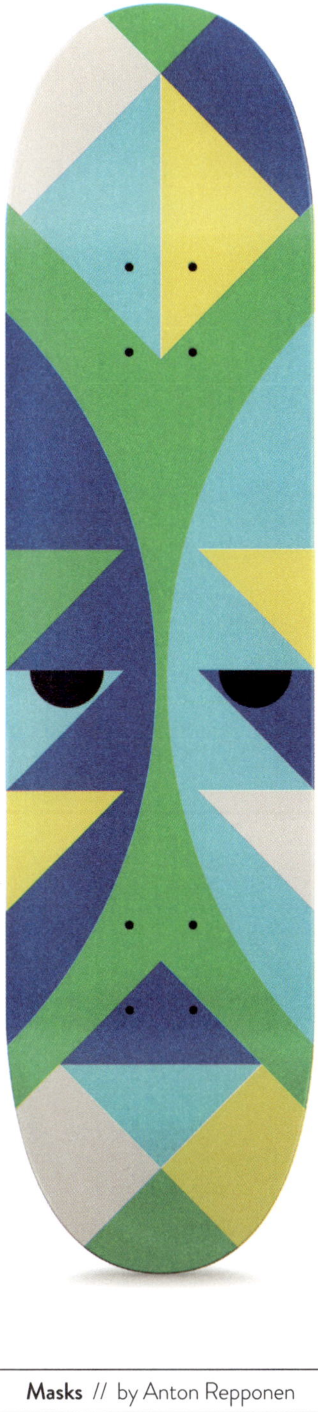

Masks // by Anton Repponen

114

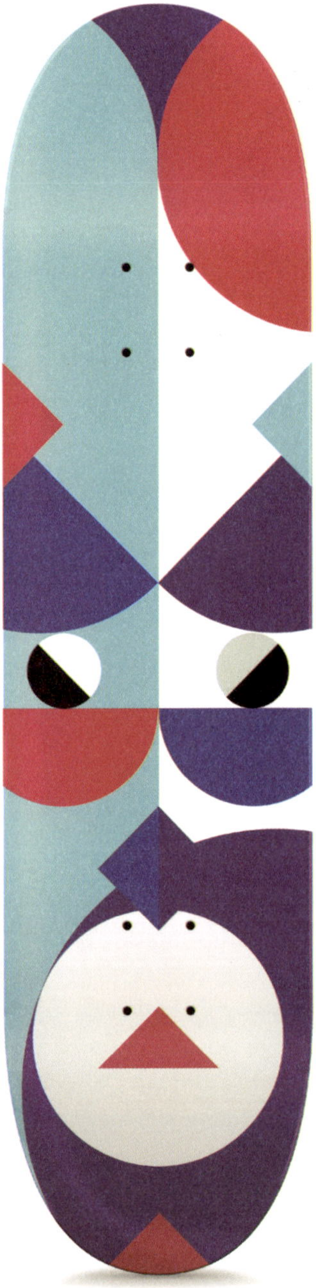

Masks // by Anton Repponen

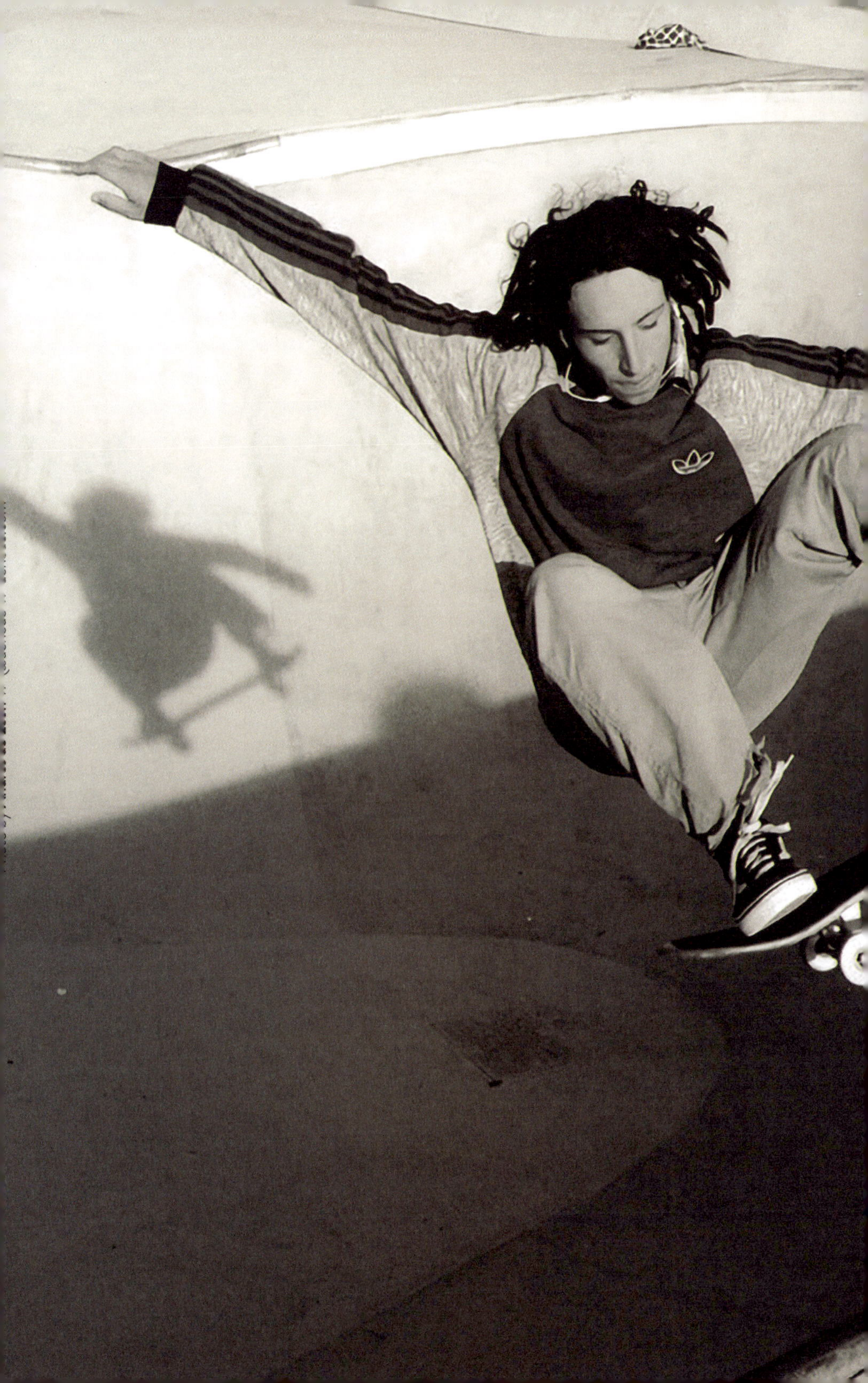

Erik Marinovich

ErikMarinovich.com

Erik Marinovich is a San Francisco based lettering artist and designer, and is a co-founder of Friends of Type. He has drawn letters, logos and type for nice folks big and small across the globe. During his free time you'll find him still drawing letters with his son and daughter.

Erik Marinovich es un escritor y diseñador con sede en San Francisco, y es cofundador de Friends of Type. Ha dibujado logotipos y tipografías de diferentes estilos, para personas de todo el mundo. Durante su tiempo libre lo encontrarás dibujando letras con su hijo e hija.

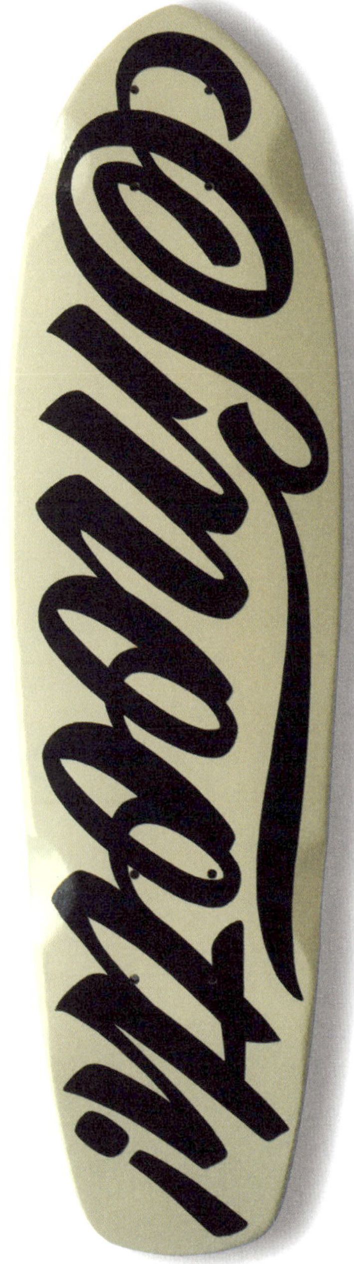

Smooth // by Erik Marinovich // for Ride On PDX

Adrià Ventura

www.adriaventura.com

Adrià Ventura is a graphic designer from Barcelona. He mainly works on brand graphic identity projects but he is always open to new projects.

His design is characterized by a balance between handmade and digital work; between the involuntary texture and the minimalism perfection. Always looking to satisfy the client's need using creativity, concept, humor, tech thoroughness and escaping from stereotypes and deciduous trends.

Adrià has been skating on a streetboard (or snakeboard) for 15 years. He started painting his own boards. While he was studying design he kept doing it with better resources (such as screenprinting). Adrià has created a whole brand and printed some boards for his college final project. After that, he wanted to work for real brands so he promoted himself in the industry. Since then he has been designing boards, wheels, merchandising, brands and so on. This kind of projects are not making him rich, but he really enjoys skating something he designed.

Adrià Ventura es un diseñador gráfico de Barcelona. Trabaja principalmente en proyectos de identidad gráfica de marca, pero siempre está abierto a nuevos proyectos.

Su diseño se caracteriza por un equilibrio entre trabajo hecho a mano y digital; Entre la textura involuntaria y la perfección minimalista. Siempre buscando satisfacer la necesidad del cliente utilizando creatividad, concepto, humor, rigurosidad tecnológica y escapar de los estereotipos y deciduous trends.

Adrià ha estado patinando en un streetboard (o snakeboard) durante 15 años. Comenzó a pintar sus propias tablas, mientras estudiaba diseño así que siguió haciéndolo cada vez con más recursos (como la serigrafía). Para su proyecto final en la universidad, creó una marca entera. Después de eso, su deseo era el trabajar para marcas reales por lo que se promovió a sí mismo en la industria. Desde entonces, ha creado el diseño de tablas, ruedas, merchandising, marcas y así sucesivamente. Este tipo de proyectos no le están haciendo rico, pero para él es un placer poder gozar del patinaje con algo diseñado por él.

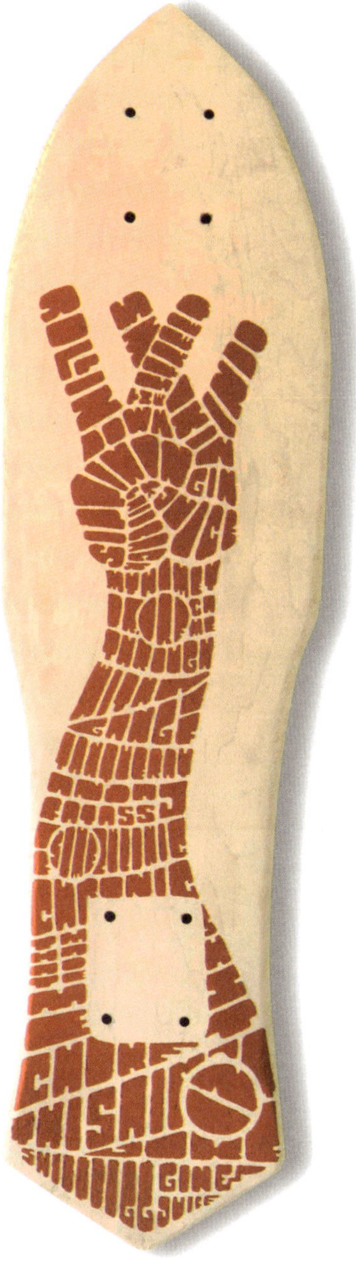

Gin & Juice // by Adrià Ventura

Handpainted board for Reskate Collective.
I designed the lettering based on the Gin & Juice Snoop Dogg's song.

Basik

www.basik.it	instagram: @basik

Basik has developed his personal style switching from spray paint to a broader range of media over the years, while mixing his original approach of graffiti writer with inspirations from Italian medieval and renaissance art masters onward, as well as influences from modern, contemporary art and graphic design.

His late figurative works focus especially on hands' gestures and take inspiration from distinctive traits in popular culture, religious iconography and symbolism.

Basik ha desarrollado su estilo personal de pasar de la pintura en aerosol a una gama más amplia de medios de comunicación a lo largo de los años, mientras que mezcla su enfoque original del escritor de graffiti con inspiraciones de los maestros italianos del arte medieval y renacentista en adelante, así como influencias de arte moderno y contemporáneo y diseño gráfico.

Sus últimas obras figurativas se centran especialmente en los gestos de las manos y se inspiran en rasgos distintivos de la cultura popular, la iconografía religiosa y el simbolismo.

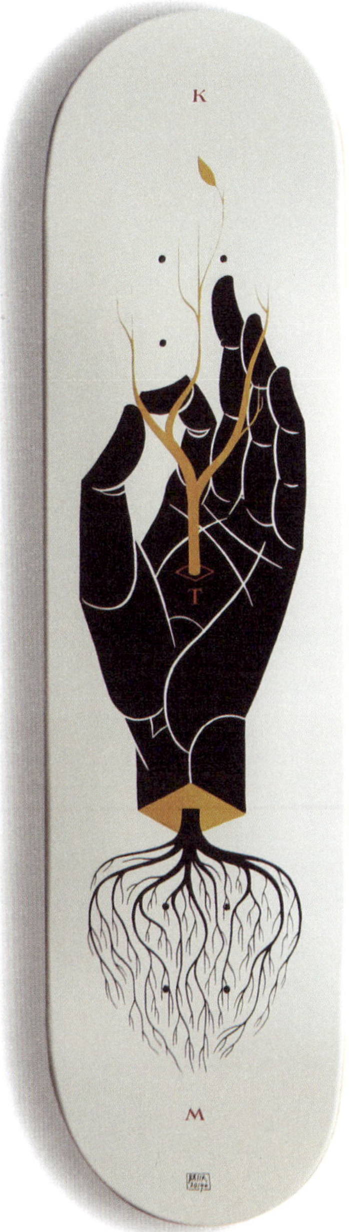

A Path Of Struggle Through A Kingdom And Its Crown // by Basik // for bonobolabo.com

The subject takes inspiration from the Sephirot of the Tree of Life, the ten emanations of Kabbalah, using elements of popular culture –in this case mystic beliefs– as metaphors part of a contemporary piece.

Andreas Preis

andreaspreis.com

Andreas Preis was born deep in the Bavarian Forest in the south of Germany, where he soon discovered his weakness for drawing and colors. After planning to become a »painter without a boss« since he was about 5 years old, he graduated from Georg-Simon-Ohm University and soon started to work on graphics for skate- and longboards, especially with Landyachtz. His skill set includes illustration, murals, tape art and live paintings as well as the different areas of traditional communications design like typography, logo design, icon design and art direction.

Andreas Preis is currently living and working in Berlin.

Andreas Preis nació en la profundidad del bosque bávaro en el sur de Alemania, donde pronto descubrió su debilidad por el dibujo y los colores. Se graduó en la Universidad Georg-Simon-Ohm y pronto comenzó a trabajar en gráficos para skate y longboards, especialmente con Landyachtz. Su conjunto de habilidades incluye ilustración, murales, arte de cinta y pinturas en vivo, así como las diferentes áreas de diseño de comunicaciones tradicionales como la tipografía, diseño de logotipos, diseño de iconos y dirección de arte.

Andreas Preis actualmente vive y trabaja en Berlín.

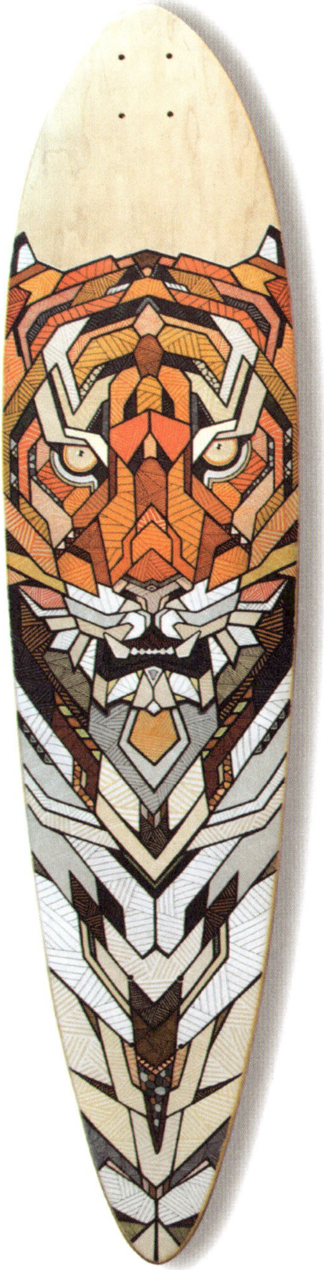

123

Tiger // by Andreas Preis

Hand-Painted

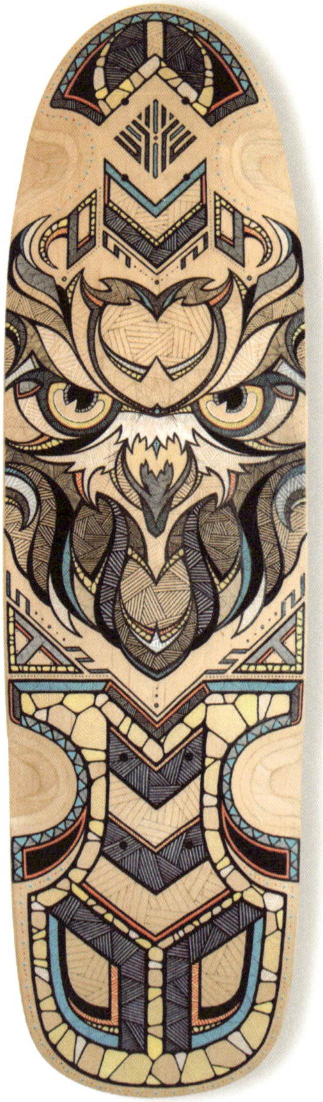

Owl // by Andreas Preis // for Landyachtz

Hand-Painted

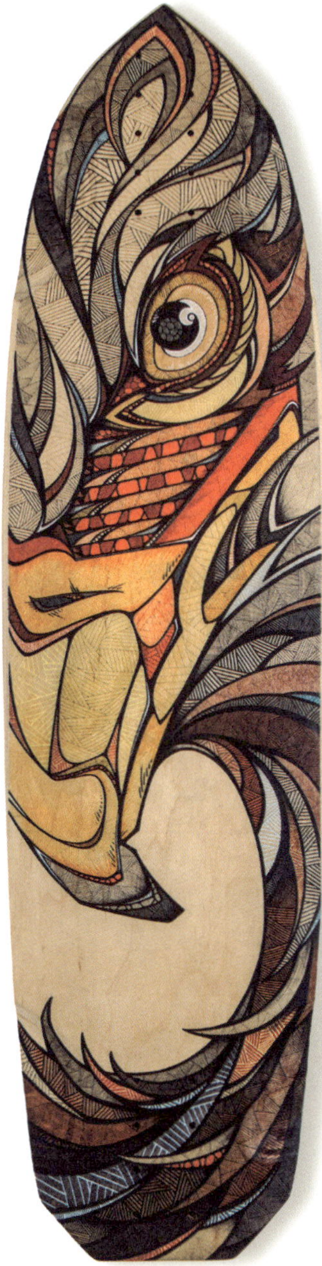

Eagle Close Up // by Andreas Preis

Hand-Painted

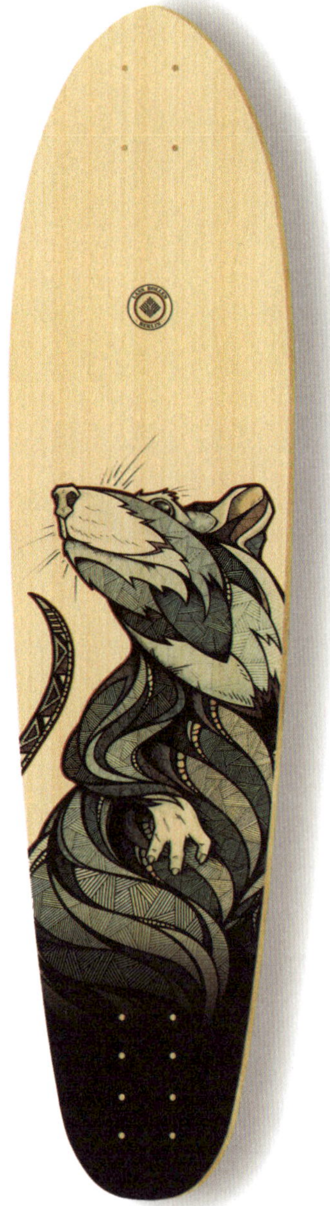

Animals of Berlin // by Andreas Preis // for LassRollen

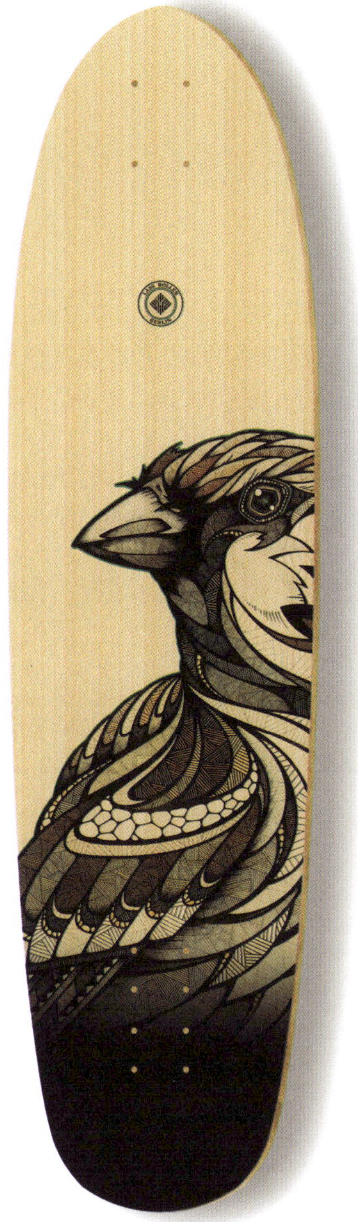

Animals of Berlin // by Andreas Preis // for LassRollen

Studio Kronk

www.studiokronk.com	instagram: @studiokronk

Studio Kronk is a semi-fictional atelier based somewhere on earth. The atelier was established by Kris "Kronk" Hewitt in 2010 and has dedicated itself to exploring spirited creative solutions for humans of all shapes and sizes, making beyond awesome products, and finding the perfect balance of logic, magic and coffee.
The studio strives to constantly have adventures of creativity and find kickass ways to use graphic art, karma and good ol' brainpower to push client and self-initiated work into new, fun and exciting realms.

Estudio Kronk es un taller semi-ficticio con sede en algún lugar en la tierra. El taller fue creado por Kris "Kronk" Hewitt en 2010 y se ha dedicado a explorar soluciones creativas espirituales para los seres humanos de todas las formas y tamaños, encontrando el equilibrio perfecto entre la lógica, la magia y el café.
El estudio se esfuerza por tener constantemente aventuras de creatividad y encontrar maneras de usar arte gráfico, karma y buena capacidad mental para empujar al cliente y al trabajo iniciado en nuevos, divertidos y excitantes reinos.

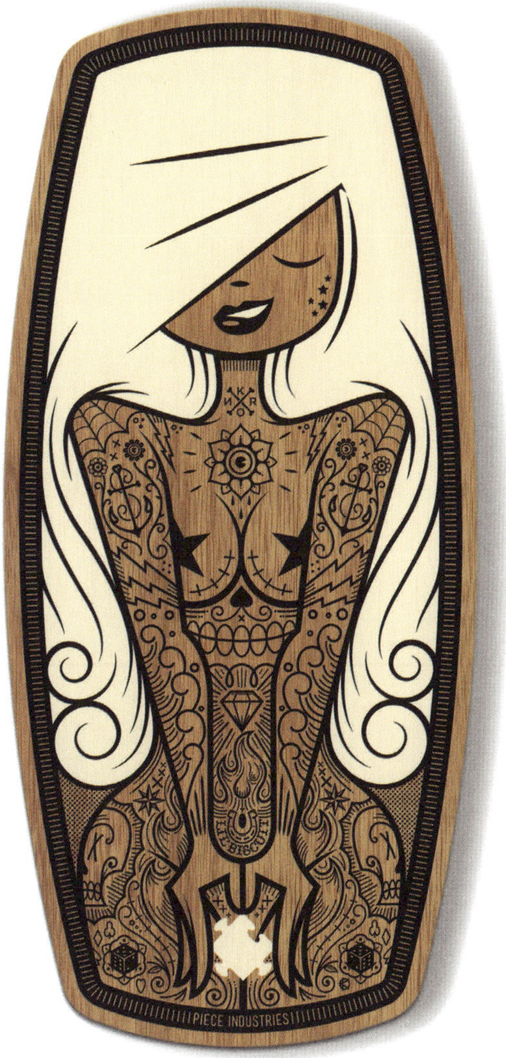

Lil Biscuit // by Studio Kronk // for pieceindustries.co.za

129

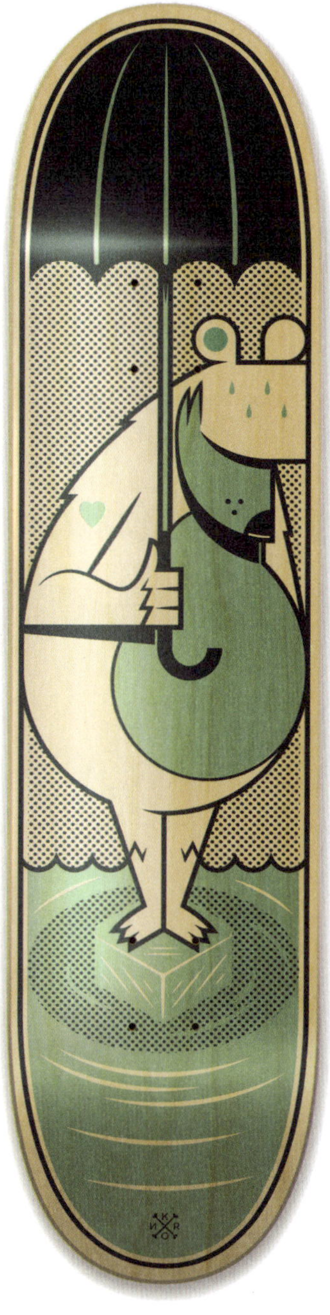

Saddest Summer Ever // by Studio Kronk // for bordobello.com

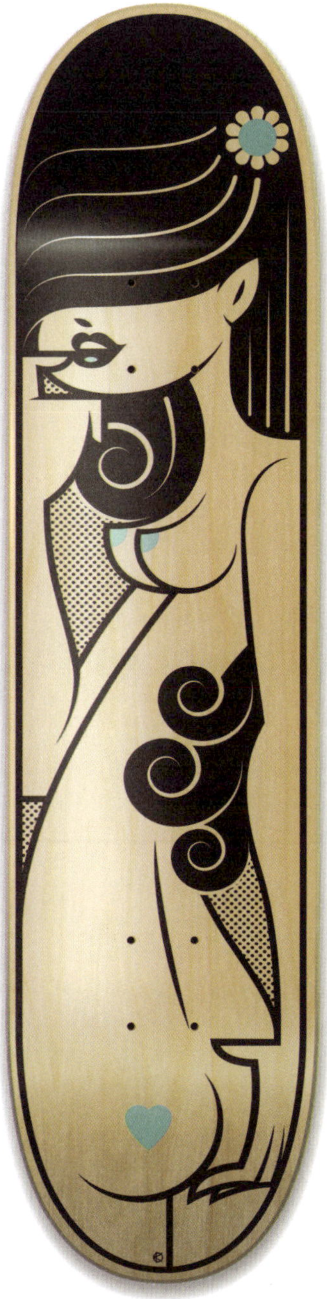

Tail Grab can be attributed // by Studio Kronk // for bordobello.com

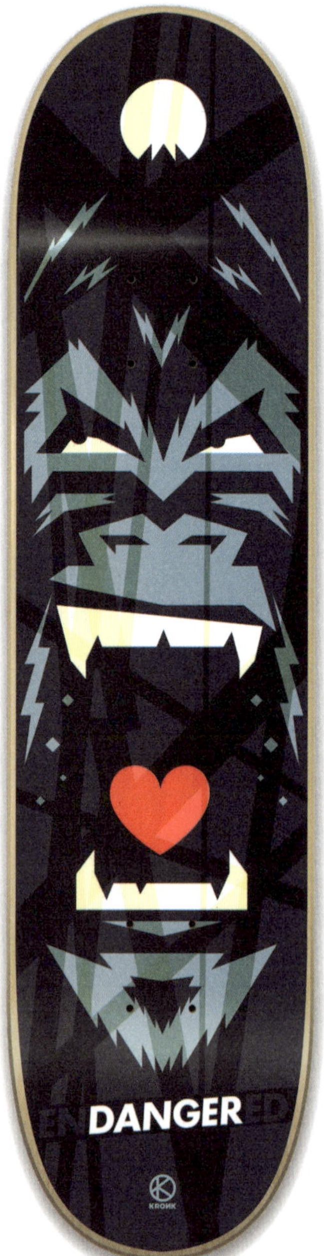

enDANGERed // by Studio Kronk

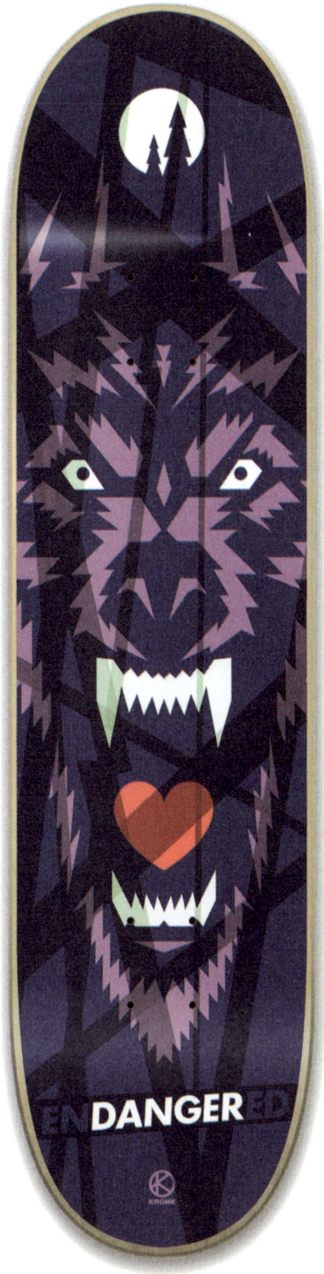

enDANGERed // by Studio Kronk

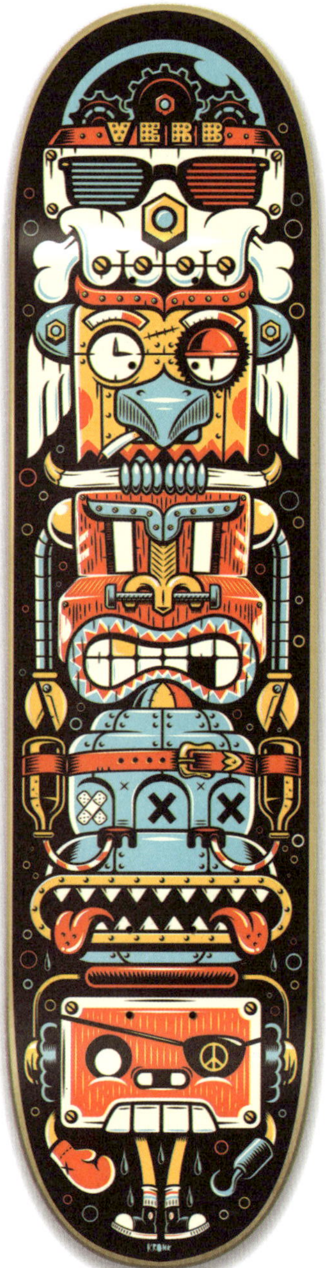

Totem of Trouble // by Studio Kronk // for weareverb.com

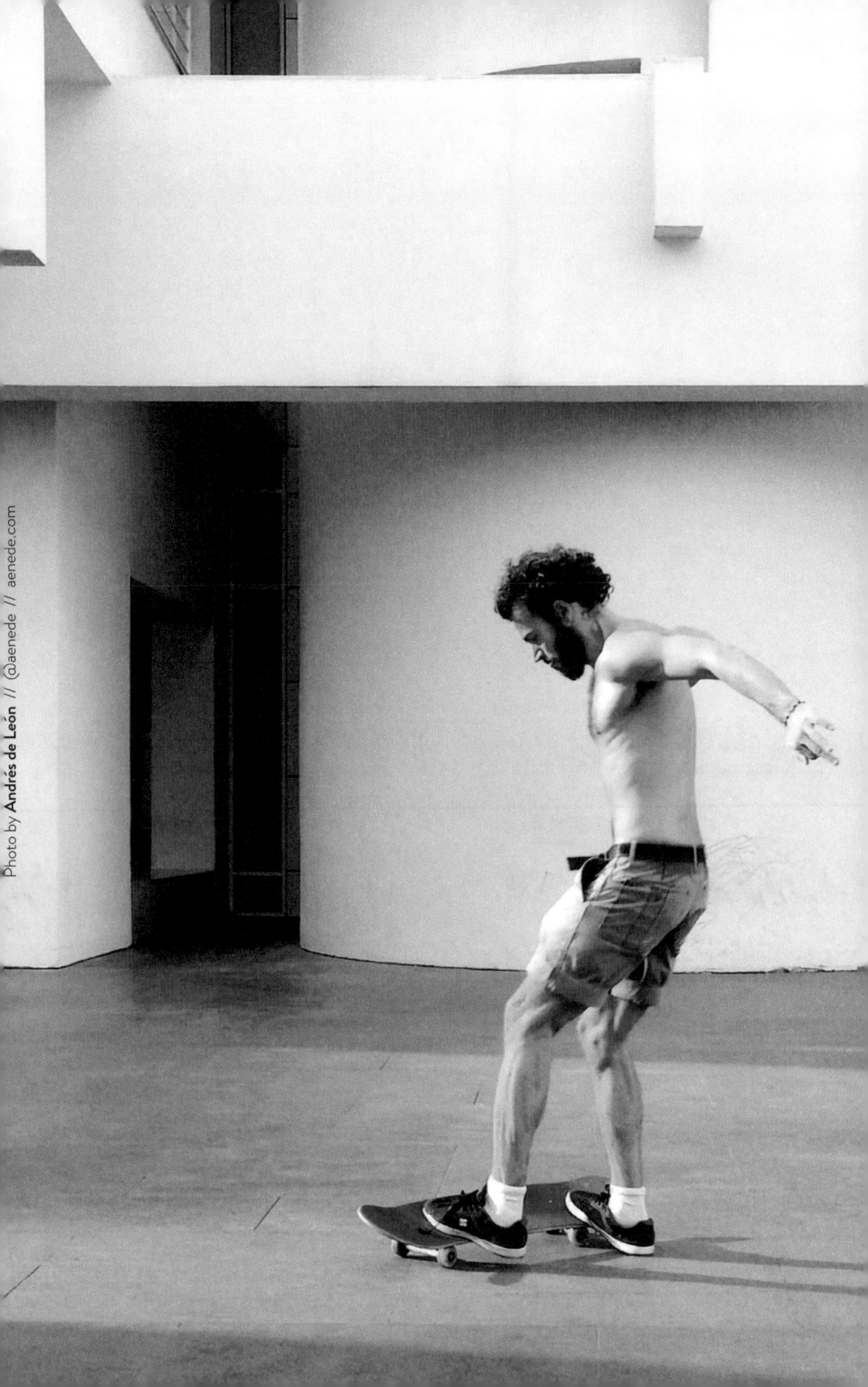

Photo by **Andrés de León** // @aenede // aenede.com

Nikita Kaun

sunturnsintowater.tumblr.com | instagram: @nikitakaun

Nikita Kaun was born in 1993, self taught artist, based out of Saint-Petersburg, Russia. He started to work commercially in 2013, since then worked with brands as Absolut, Dillinger Escape Plan, Sourvein, Being As An Ocean, ROME Snowboards.

"His style is a mixture of predominantly black and white realistically rendered forms falling into a dreamlike darkness with minimal pops of color." - Juxtapoz

Nikita Kaun nació en 1993, artista autodidacta, con sede en San Petersburgo, Rusia. Comenzó a trabajar comercialmente en 2013, desde entonces trabaja con marcas como Absolut, Dillinger Escape Plan, Sourvein, Ser Como Un Océano, ROME Snowboards.

"Su estilo es una mezcla de formas predominantemente negras y blancas de formas realistas que caen en una oscuridad de ensueño con mínimos estallidos de color." - Juxtapoz

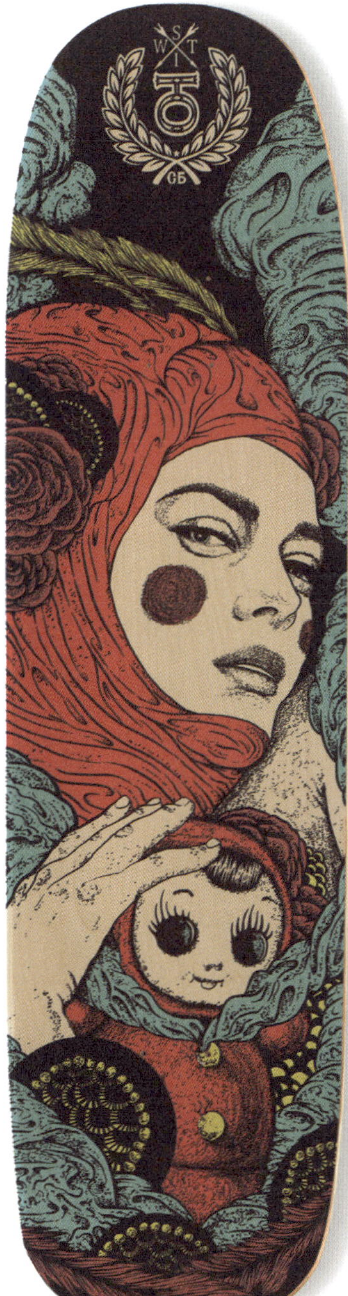

DeadGirl // by Nikita Kaun

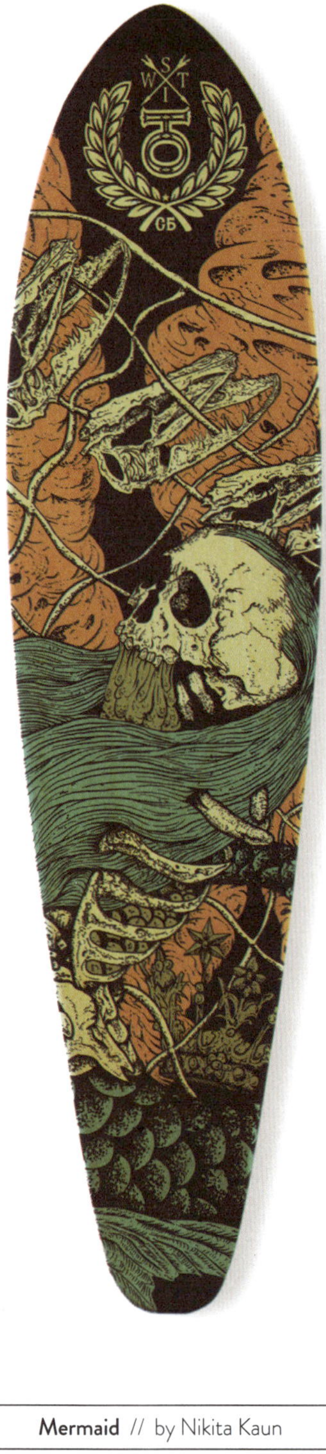

138

Mermaid // by Nikita Kaun

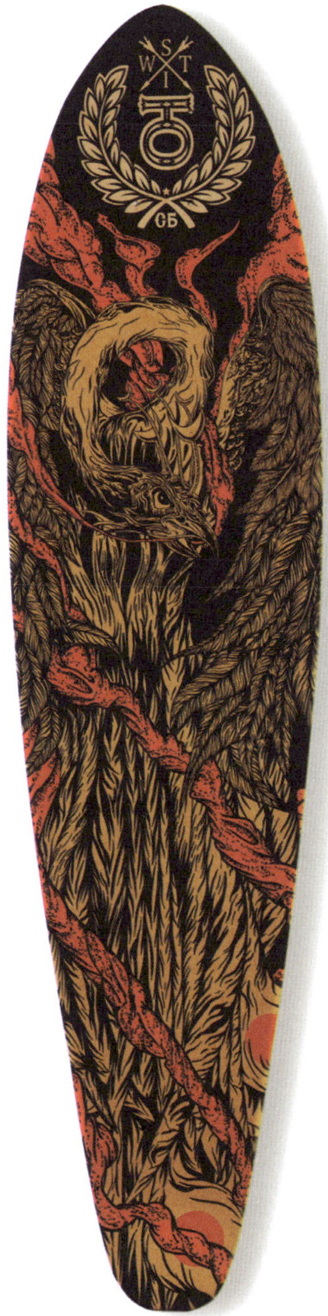

Zhar // by Nikita Kaun

Antero Nuutinen

www.anteronuutinen.com	instagram: @anteronuutinen

Antero Nuutinen thinks that he is more graphic designer that illustrator. But his passion is lettering. In particular Script lettering. His favourite tool is pointed brush and brush pens, but he likes to experiment with all kinds of writing tools. He spends lot of time with his projects to make them as good as he can.

Antero Nuutinen piensa que es más diseñador gráfico que ilustrador. Pero su pasión es el lettering. En particular Script lettering. Su herramienta favorita son los pinceles puntiagudos y las plumas, pero le gusta experimentar con todo tipo de herramientas de escritura. Pasa mucho tiempo con sus proyectos para hacerlos tan perfectos como pueda.

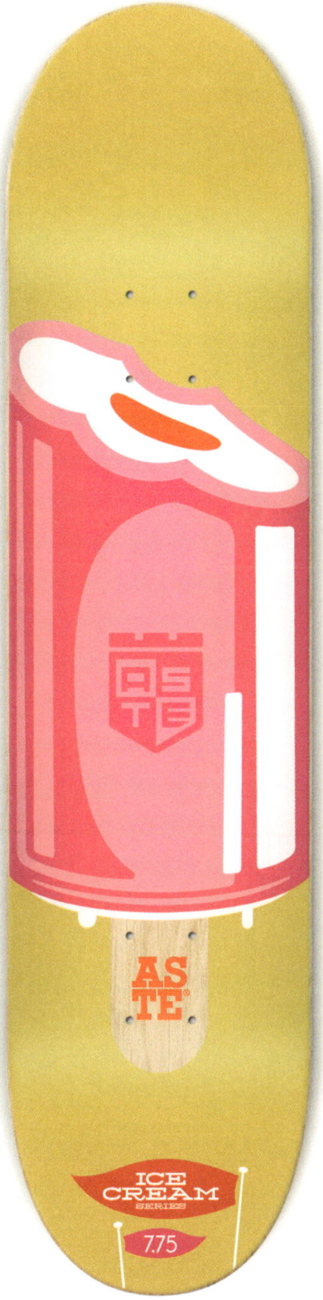

IceCream // by Antero Nuutinen

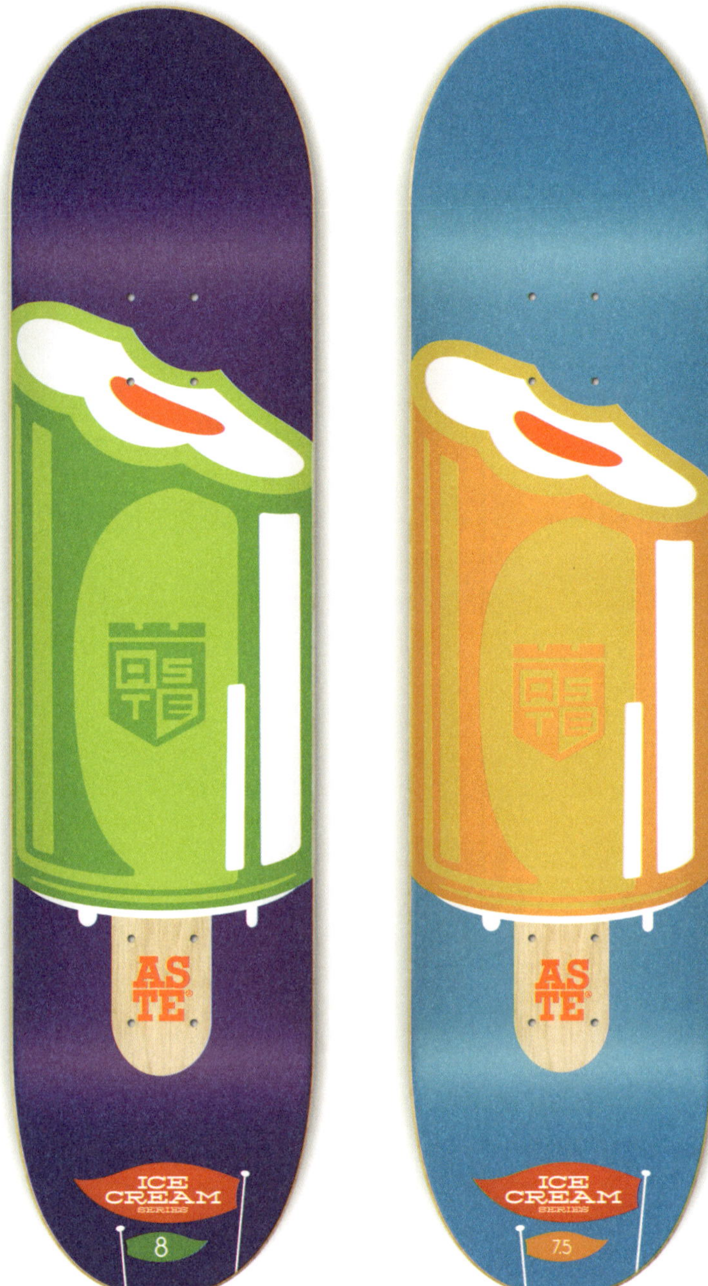

IceCream // by Antero Nuutinen

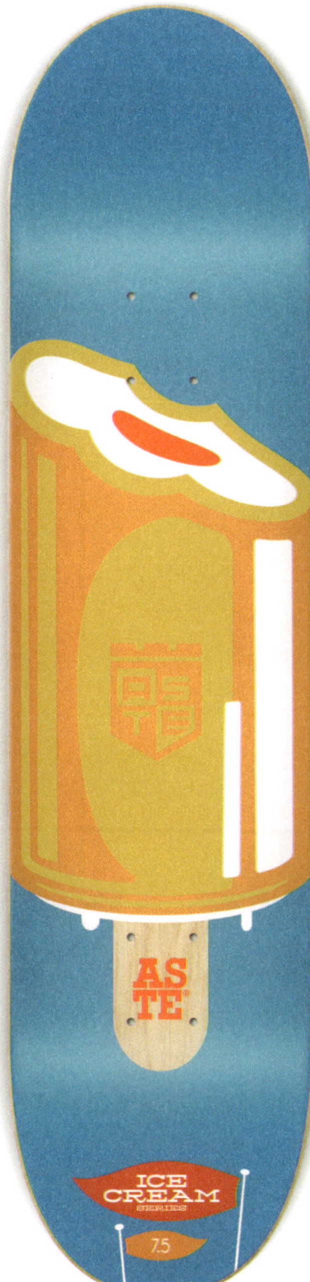

IceCream // by Antero Nuutinen

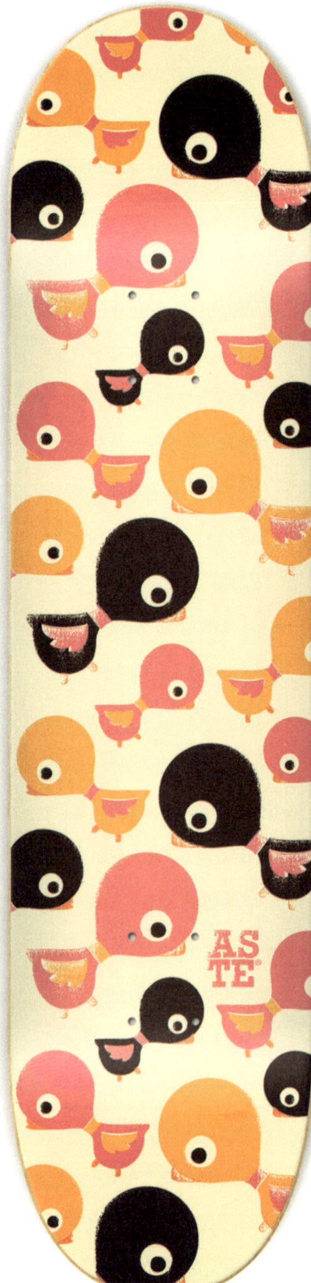

Duck // by Antero Nuutinen

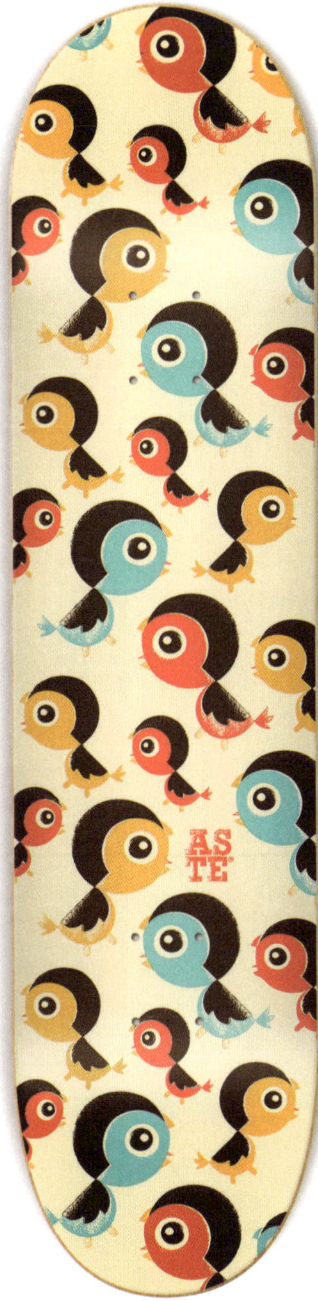

Birdie // by Antero Nuutinen

Idem

idem.brussels

Idem is a graphic artist / illustrator from Brussels who is passionate about street-art, typography, comics...
He finds inspiration from different styles that he mixes with each other.

He particularly likes to switch up the surfaces on which he works: canvas, walls, skateboards, cars, T-shirts, etc. This allows him to look into different horizons and not belong to ONE style. While exploring various techniques, styles and media, idem is continuously searching but also keeping his concrete and figurative style balanced.

Idem es un artista gráfico / ilustrador de Bruselas que es un apasionado del street-art, la tipografía, el cómic...
Encuentra la inspiración en diferentes estilos que mezcla entre sí.

En particular, le gusta cambiar las superficies sobre las que trabaja: lienzo, paredes, skateboards, coches, camisetas, etc. Esto le permite mirar en diferentes horizontes y no pertenecer a un solo estilo. Mientras explora diversas técnicas, y medios, está continuamente buscando pero también manteniendo un equilibrio entre lo concreto y lo figurativo.

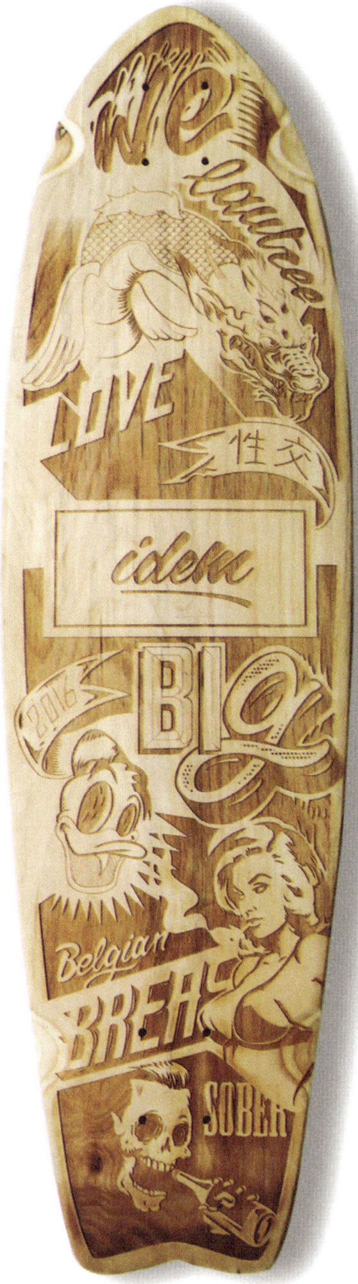

by Idem

Laser cut

Kendrick Kidd

www.kendrickkidd.com

Kendrick Kidd is a proud native of sunny Florida where he grew up skating & surfing since the age of 5. He's been designing professionally for the last 18 years, and have a healthy love for packaging, branding, and illustration. He is currently working as a Associate Creative Director at an advertising agency in Jacksonville, FL called Shepherd, and he also runs a small design & screen printing business during nights and weekends. The last 7 years Kendrick has focused much of his energy on design, and branding for craft breweries, action sports companies, and editorial publications. With some hard work, and a little luck he hopes to continue along this path for as long as humanly possible.

Kendrick Kidd es un orgulloso nativo de la soleada Florida donde creció patinando y practicando surf desde los 5 años de edad. Ha estado diseñando profesionalmente durante los últimos 18 años y tiene un amor sano por el packaging, el branding y la ilustración. Actualmente trabaja como Director Creativo Asociado en una agencia de publicidad en Jacksonville, FL llamada Shepherd, y también dirige un pequeño negocio de diseño y serigrafía durante las noches y los fines de semana. Los últimos 7 años Kendrick ha centrado gran parte de su energía en el diseño, y la creación de marcas para cervecerías, compañías de deportes de acción, y publicaciones editoriales. Con un poco de trabajo duro, y un poco de suerte espera continuar en este camino durante el tiempo que sea humanamente posible.

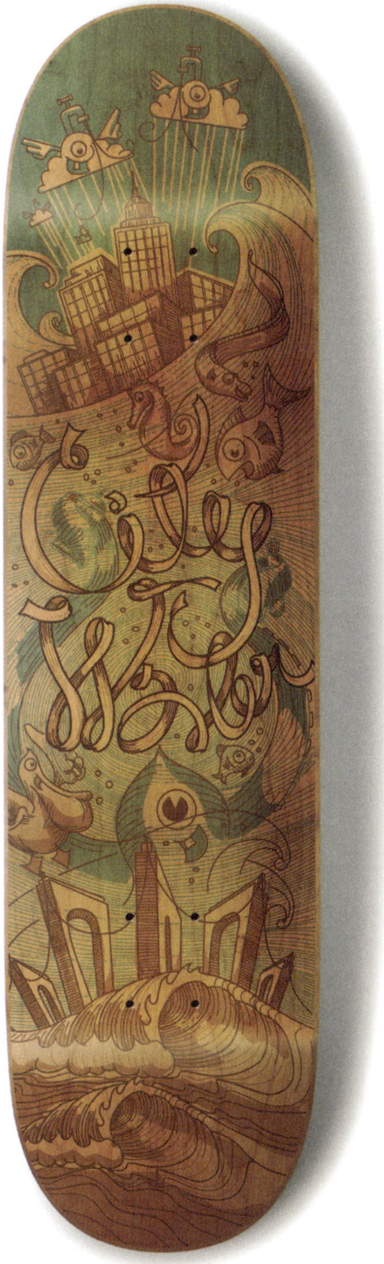

City Water Deck // by Kendrick Kidd

The City Water deck was a private commission. The direction was to combine urban living with an ocean themes. The result was a playful mono weight illustration of a city underwater.

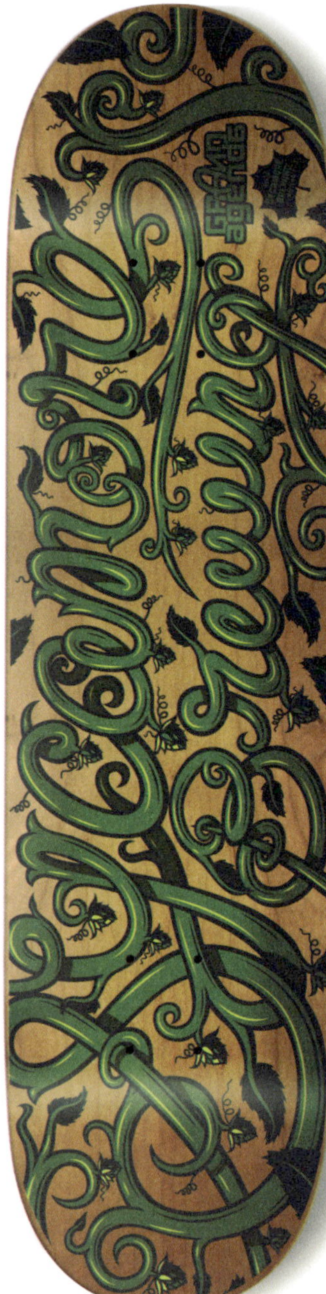

Sycamore Brewing Deck // by Kendrick Kidd // for Grand Agenda

The art direction was wide open, only that the final product represent brewery in a positive light.

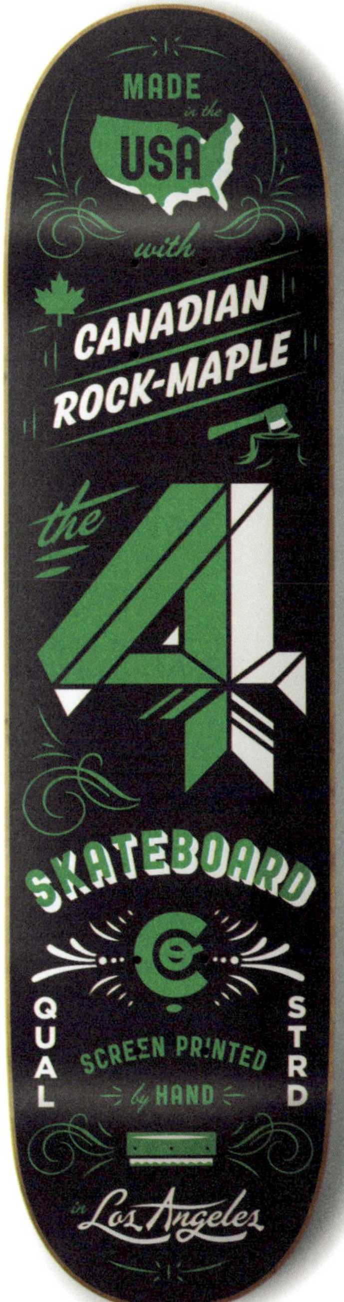

Sign Painter Deck // by Kendrick Kidd // for The 4 skateboard company

The Sign Painter deck series was created to emphasize the quality & care.

Junichi Tsuneoka

www.stubbornsideburn.com

Junichi Tsuneoka was born and raised in Japan and, upon graduating Waseda University in Tokyo, arrived in the US at the end of the 20th Century. Being a graphic designer at Modern Dog Design Co. for six years really made a great impact on Junichi's design career. Because of that experience, Junichi established a style often recognized as "California Roll Stylie," the result of both a visual and conceptual fusion of Japanese pop culture and American urban culture. He founded Studio Stubborn Sideburn to broaden his visual communication and to employ his visual language in art, illustration, and design. Junichi's pieces possess highly communicative, assertive graphics, and contain clear signs pointing back to his strong design background.

Junichi Tsuneoka nació y creció en Japón, al graduarse por la Universidad Waseda en Tokio, llegó a los Estados Unidos a finales del siglo XX. Es diseñador gráfico en Modern Dog Design Co. durante seis años realmente provocó un gran impacto en su carrera. Debido a esa experiencia, Junichi estableció un estilo a menudo reconocido como "California Roll Stylie", el resultado de una fusión visual y conceptual de la cultura pop japonesa y la cultura urbana americana. Fundó Studio Stubborn Sideburn para ampliar su comunicación visual y emplear su lenguaje visual en el arte, la ilustración y el diseño. Las piezas de Junichi poseen gráficos altamente comunicativos, asertivos, y contienen señales claras que apuntan de nuevo a su fondo fuerte del diseño.

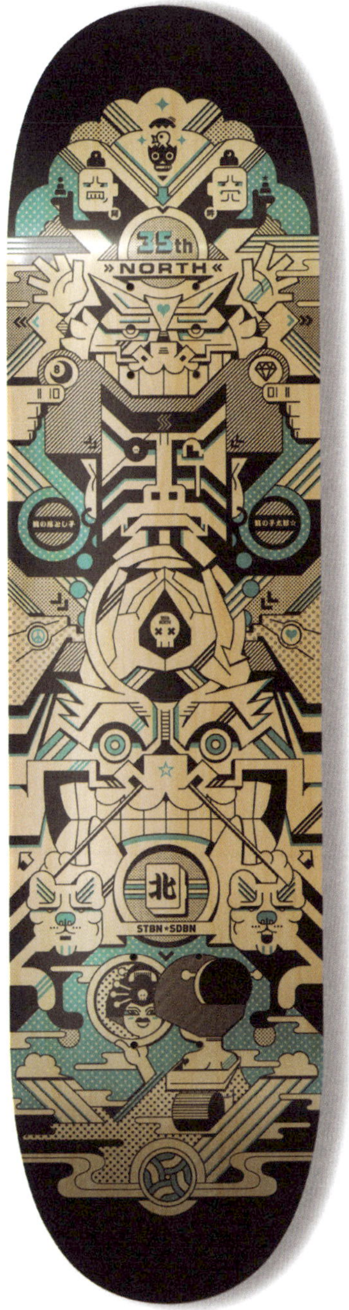

35th Skateboard // by Junichi Tsuneoka

This was designed as a limited edition skate board for a local skate store in Seattle.

Travis Gillan

TravisGillan.com	instagram: @TravisGillan

Born in Michigan, Travis now resides and freelances in Denver, Colorado. Drawing from the beauty and awe the natural world provides, Travis' art blooms forward with lush detail and intense symbolism. Inspired by a pantheistic perspective, all aspects of his work come alive. The conscious, organic elements contrast geometric archetypes that allude to an intelligent formula behind reality's curtain. Coming from an illustration background, Travis stays true to a pen and ink approach while maintaining an engaging color palette. Working with various clients such as Pabst Brewing Company and Creature Boards, and employing his art to various mediums, Travis' art lends itself to an array of applications.

Nacido en Michigan, ahora reside y es freelance en Denver, Colorado. Dibujante de la belleza y del temor que el mundo natural proporciona, el arte de Travis florece con detalle exuberante y simbolismo intenso. Inspirado por una perspectiva panteísta, todos los aspectos de su obra cobran vida. Los elementos conscientes y los orgánicos contrastan con los arquetipos geométricos que aluden a una fórmula inteligente detrás de la cortina de la realidad. Viniendo de un fondo de la ilustración, Travis permanece fiel a un acercamiento de la pluma y de la tinta mientras que mantiene una gama de colores atractiva. Trabajando con varios clientes como Pabst Brewing Company y Creature Boards, y empleando su arte en diversos medios, su arte se presta a una gran variedad de aplicaciones.

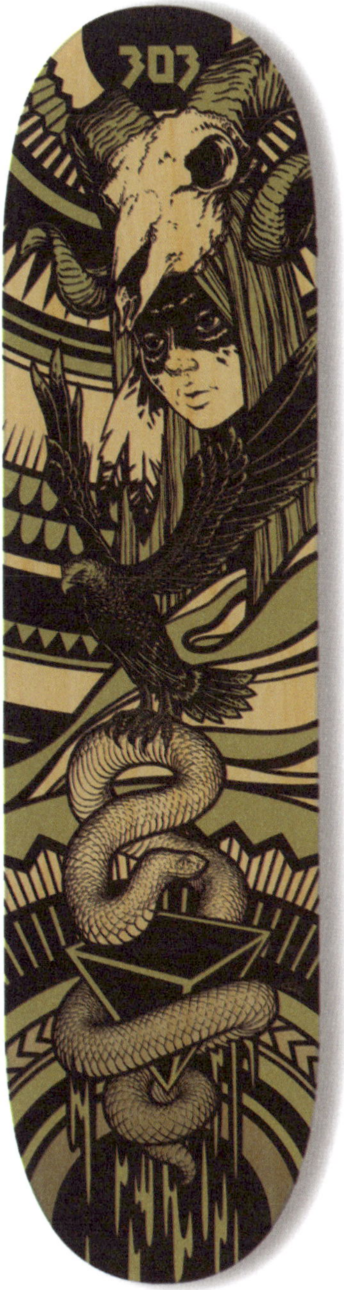

Eagle Mystic // by Travis Gillan

With these skateboards, contrasting elements of life and death are used to dissolve the veil separating them. Reality is the transcendence of polarity.

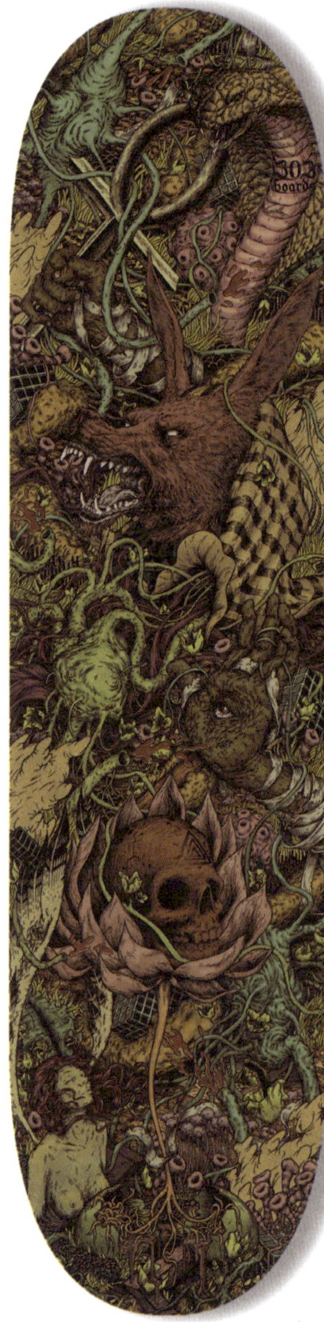

Anubis // by Travis Gillan

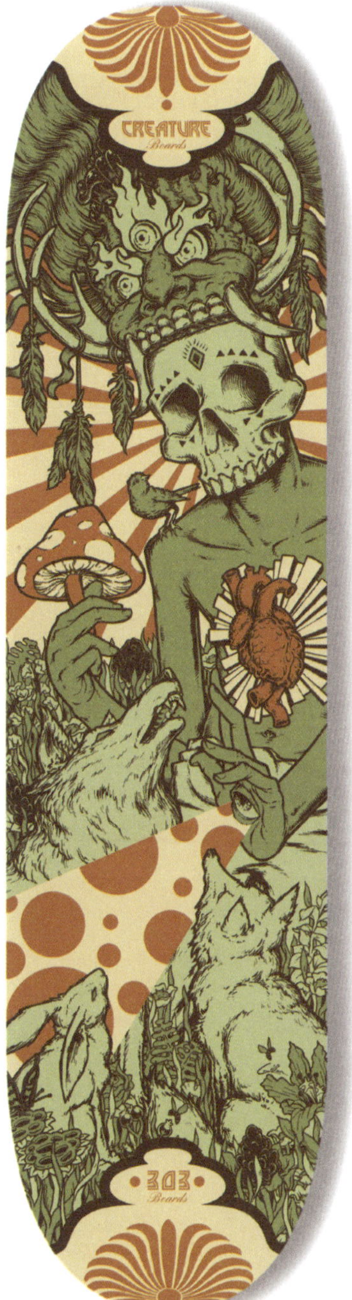

High Priest // by Travis Gillan

Jean Jullien

jeanjullien.com	instagram: @jean_jullien

Jean Jullien is a French graphic artist currently living in London and Los Angeles. Originally hailing from Nantes, he completed a graphic design degree in Quimper before moving to London, graduating from Central Saint Martins in 2008 and from the Royal College of Art in 2010. His practice ranges from illustration to photography, video, costumes, installations, books, posters and clothing to create a coherent yet eclectic body of work. His first monograph, Modern Life, was published by teNeues in October 2016.

Jean Jullien es un artista gráfico francés que actualmente vive entre Londres y Los Ángeles. Originario de Nantes, diplomado en diseño gráfico en Quimper y graduado en Central Saint Martins en 2008 y del Royal College of Art en 2010. Su práctica abarca desde la ilustración hasta la fotografía, vídeo, vestuario, instalaciones, libros, carteles y ropa para crear un cuerpo de trabajo coherente pero ecléctico. Su primera monografía, Modern Life, fue publicada por teNeues en octubre de 2016.

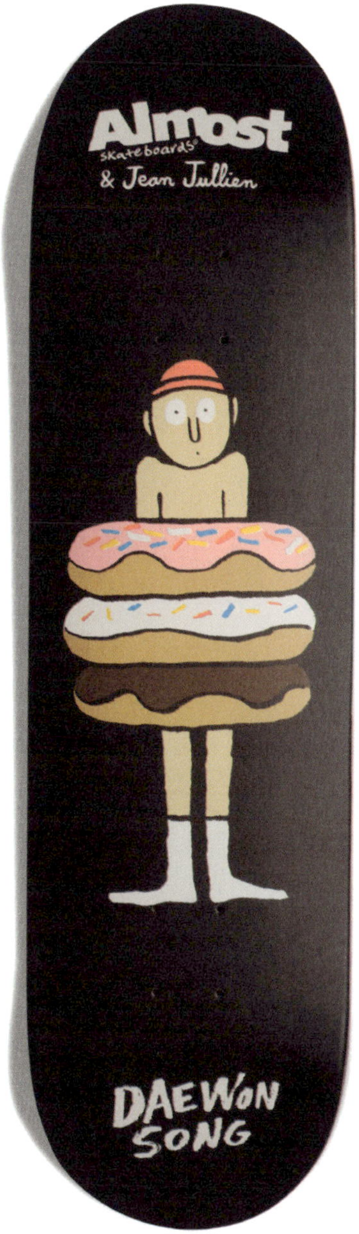

Donuts // by Jean Jullien

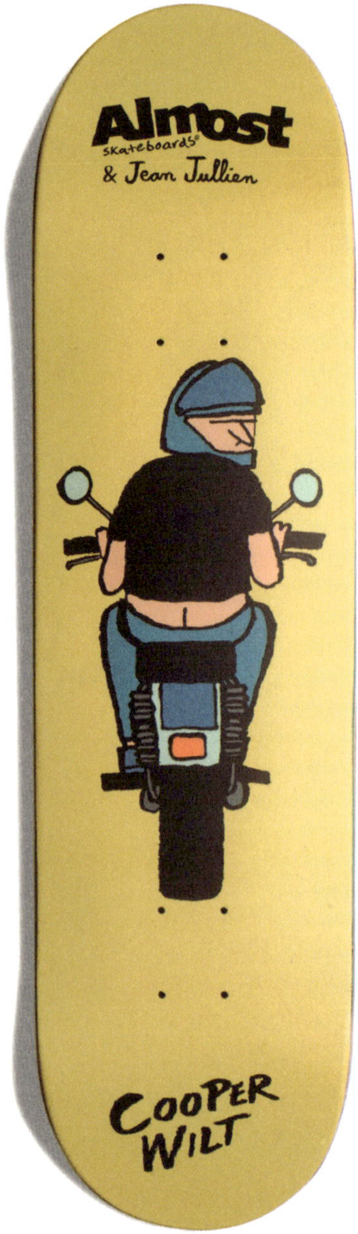

Motorcycle // by Jean Jullien

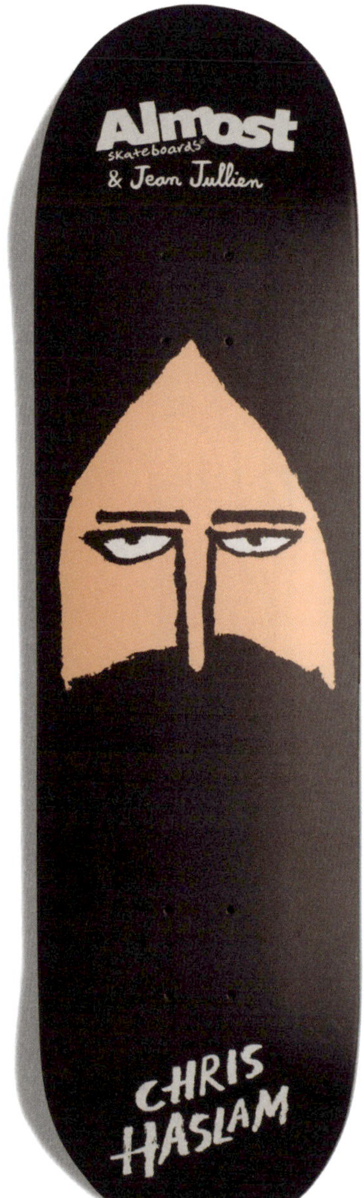

161

Lurker // by Jean Jullien

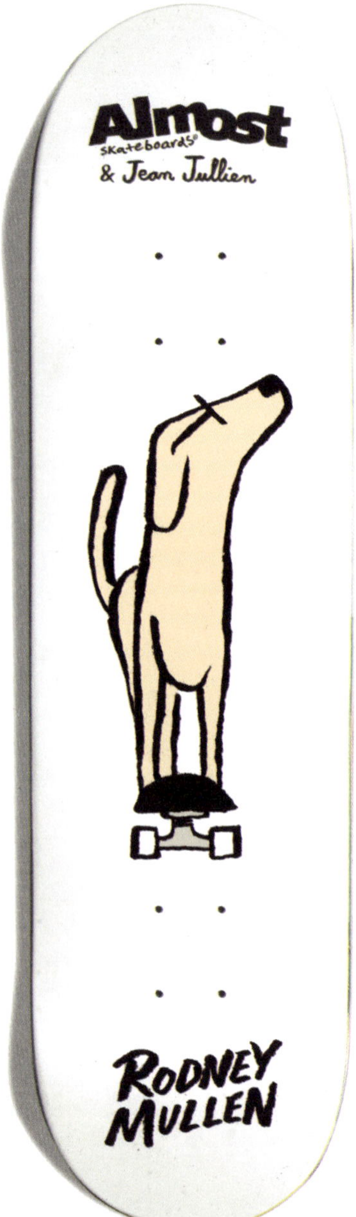

Dog // by Jean Jullien

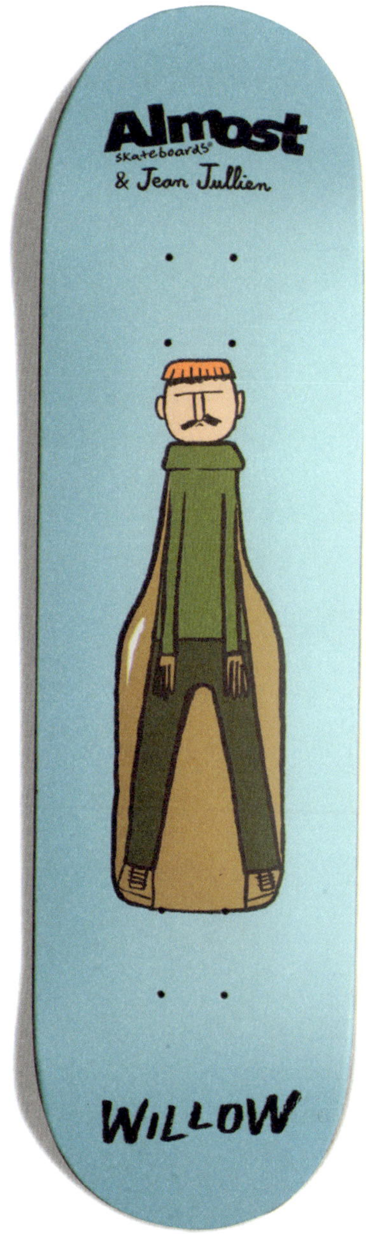

Booze // by Jean Jullien

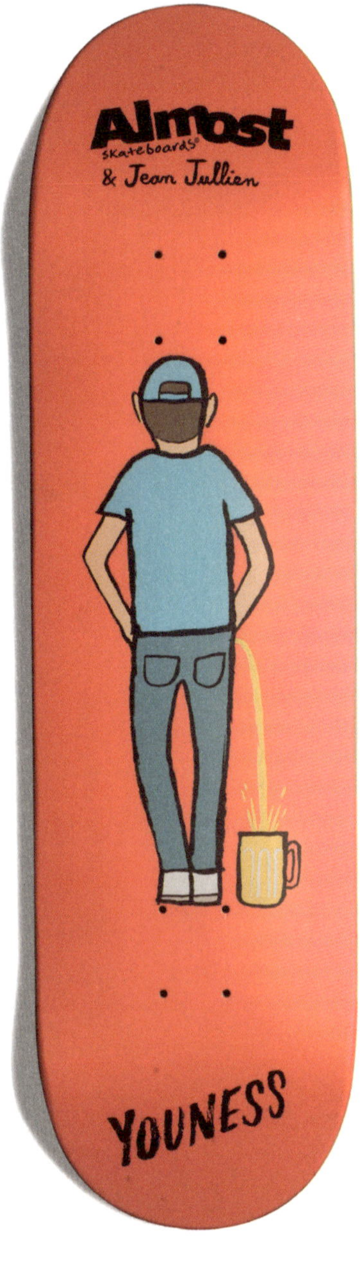

Manikin // by Jean Jullien

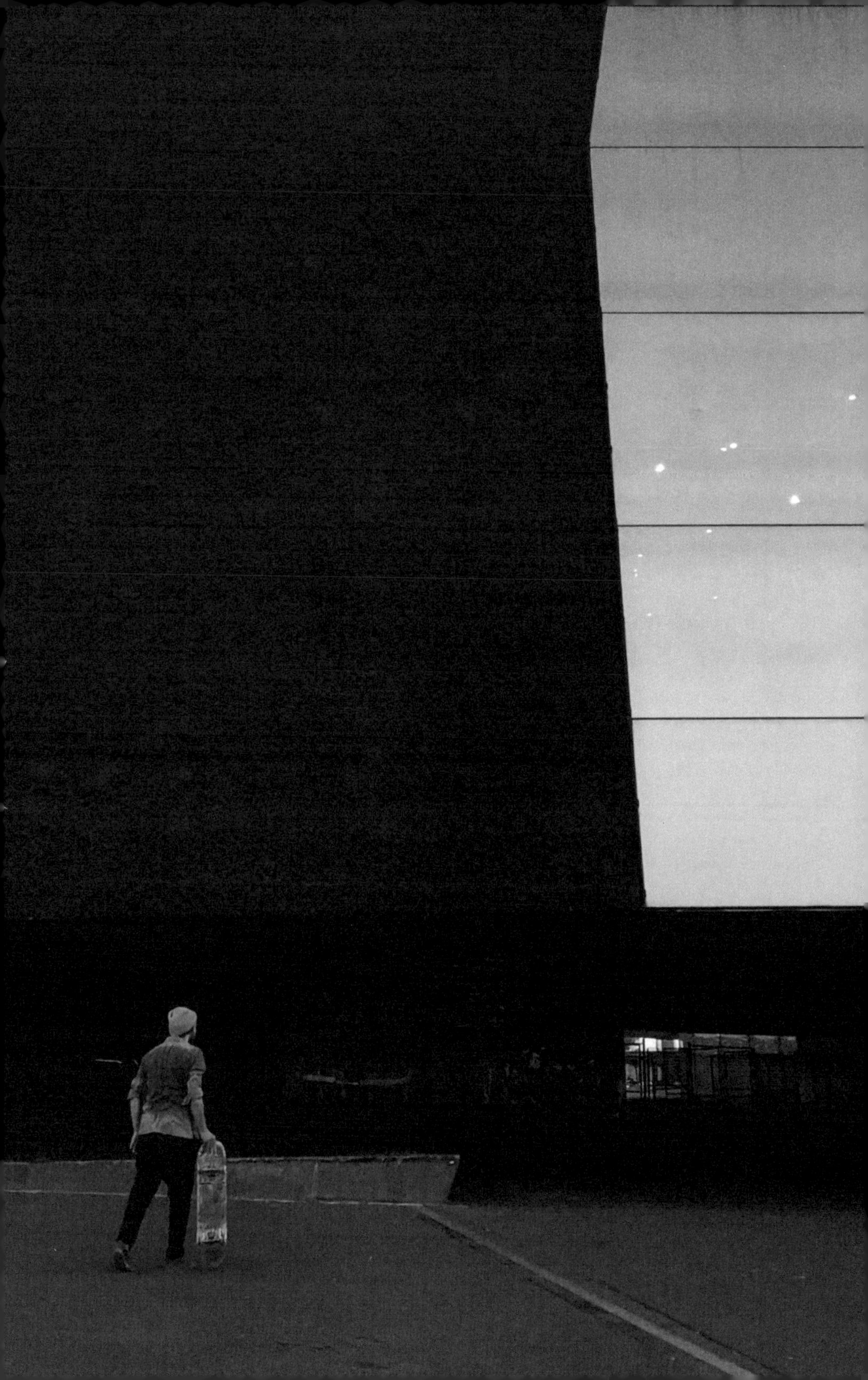

Miranda Meeks

mirandameeks.com | miranda-meeks.tumblr.com

Miranda Meeks designs and paints illustrations for clients, as well as paintings for galleries. Her work either goes on book covers, product packaging, card art, or galleries. She usually uses digital mediums to create her work, such as with Photoshop and a Wacom graphics tablet, although lately she has been branching out to more traditional methods to create oil paintings. Her main goal in her work is to combine themes of beauty with mystery and strangeness; the challenge of bridging the gap between those two themes intrigues her. Miranda believes strongly in the power of using art to connect the artist with the viewer and to communicate ideas and emotions on a personal level. When she is not creating illustrations for clients, Miranda continues to create personal work. "This is essential to maintaining momentum throughout your career."

Miranda Meeks diseña y pinta ilustraciones para clientes, así como pinturas para galerías. Su trabajo va desde las cubiertas de un libro, el packaging del producto, el diseño de arte de tarjetas, hasta exponer en galerías. Por lo general, utiliza medios digitales para crear su trabajo, como con Photoshop y una tablet gráfica Wacom, aunque últimamente se ha ramificado a los métodos más tradicionales para crear con pinturas al óleo. Su principal objetivo en su trabajo es combinar temas de belleza con misterio y extrañeza; El reto de salvar la brecha entre esos dos temas la intriga. Miranda cree firmemente en el poder de usar el arte para conectar al artista con el espectador y para comunicar ideas y emociones a un nivel personal. Cuando no está creando ilustraciones para los clientes, continúa creando trabajos personales. "Esto es esencial para mantener el impulso a lo largo de su carrera".

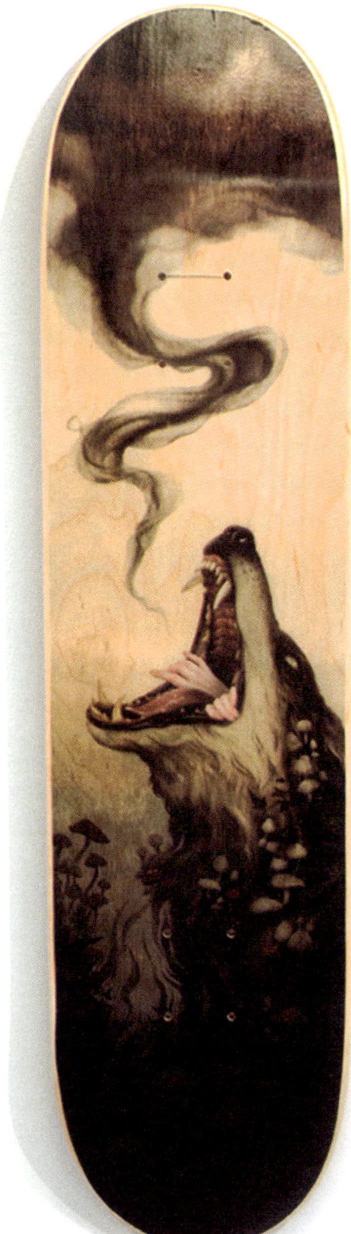

Consume // by Miranda Meeks

An image inspired by the symbolism of wolves.
It was created in photoshop then printed onto the skate deck.

Anthony Yankovic

www.anthonyyankovic.com

Anthony Yankovic is an illustrator and designer currently residing in Baltimore, MD. He has created board graphics for Alien Workshop, Foundation skateboards and several other non-reputable brands.

Anthony Yankovic es un ilustrador y diseñador que actualmente reside en Baltimore, MD. Él ha creado los gráficos de la tarjeta para Alien Workshop, skateboards para la Fundación y otras marcas no conocidas.

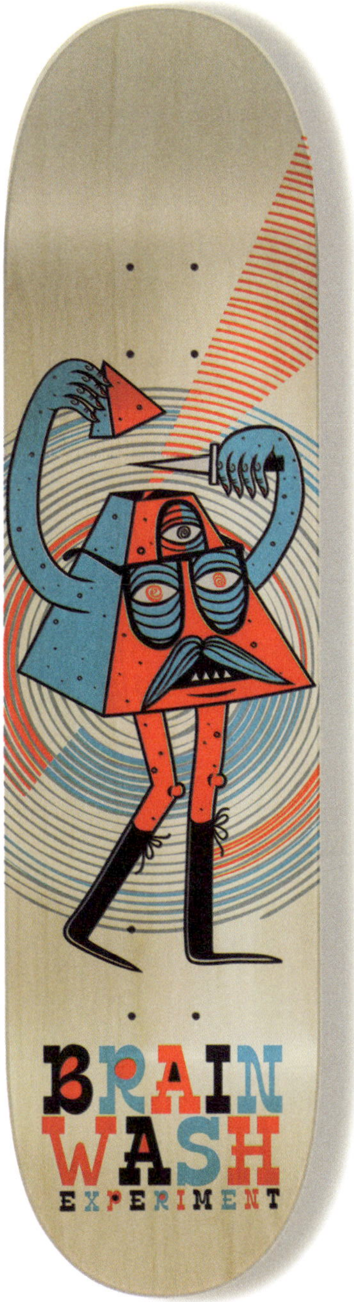

169

The Brainwash Experiment // by Anthony Yankovic

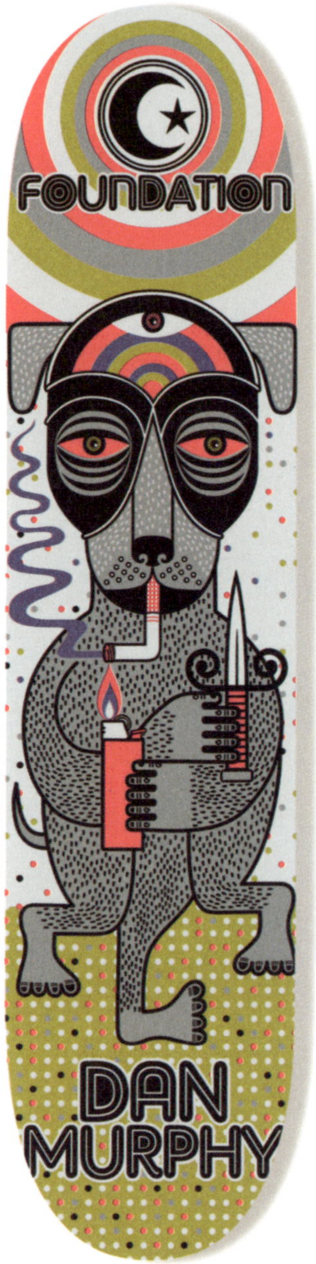

Dan Murphy // by Anthony Yankovic

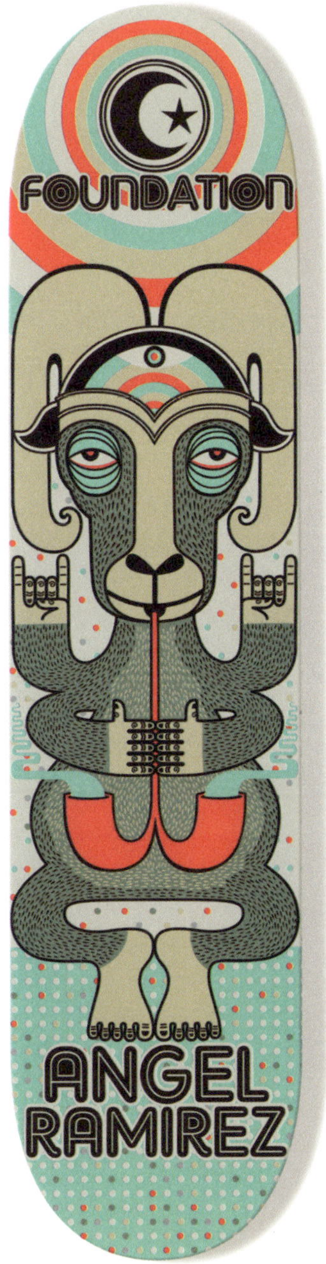

Angel Ramirez // by Anthony Yankovic

Studio Kronk

www.studiokronk.com | instagram: @studiokronk

I grew up in Muizenberg, a famous Cape Town surf area, with a strong beach style skate culture. I had always been exposed to surf and skate graphics, but my real interest in these graphics was sparked on my first visit to the local surf/skate shop to buy my first "proper" skate setup. I remember staring in awe of the use of illustration, graphic design, branding, typography, humor, satire, absurdity and low-brow style on each of the boards. Skate and surf graphics for me has always had a strong link to design and art, and these graphics can go from being modernist to punk in the same breath and that is perfectly acceptable. That for me has always meant that these cultures accept diversity as its visual voice, which has remained with me in my work. Skate and surf culture really has no one style, the act of being on a board is the style and designs just help enhance that expression and personality for each rider.

Crecí en Muizenberg, una famosa zona de surf de Ciudad del Cabo, con una fuerte cultura por el skate. Siempre ha estado vinculado a la estética gráfica del surf y el skate, pero su verdadero interés por estos gráficos se desencadenó en su primera visita a la tienda local de surf/skate para comprar por partes su primer skate. Recuerda mirar con asombro el uso de la ilustración, el diseño gráfico, el branding, la tipografía, el humor, la sátira, el absurdo y el estilo en cada una de las tablas. Los gráficos skate y surf siempre han tenido un fuerte vínculo con el diseño y el arte, los diseños pueden pasar de ser modernistas a punk en el mismo aliento y combinan perfectamente. Eso significa que estas culturas aceptan la diversidad como su voz visual, que ha permanecido en su trabajo. El skate y la cultura del surf realmente no tiene un estilo definido, los diseños de las tablas sólo ayudan a mejorar la expresión y la personalidad de cada jinete.

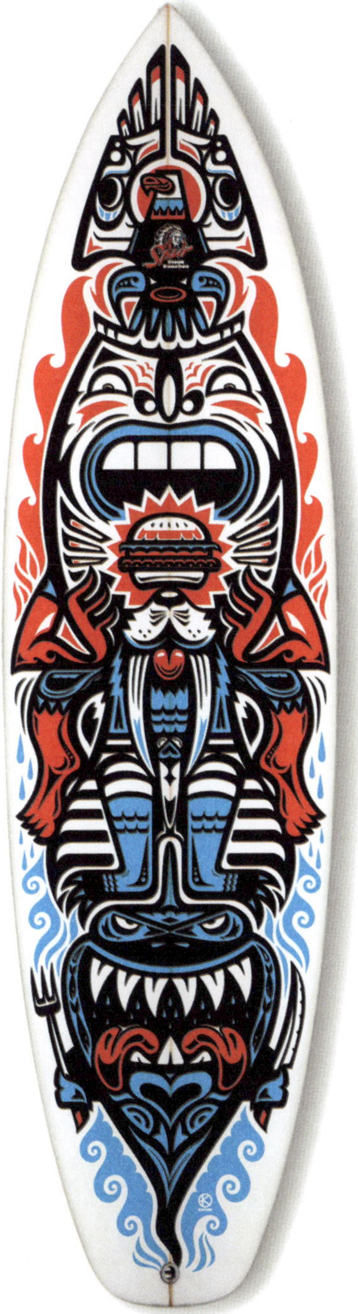

Tasty Totem // by Studio Kronk // for spur.co.za

Daniela Garreton

www.danigarreton.com

Daniela Garreton (1983*) is a Basque Country based artist. She was born in Santiago de Chile. Growing up in a deverse country with more than 4.000km of varied coastline, the sea soon became her life passion.

In 2010 Daniela moved to Europe and chose another coastal city, San Sebastian, as her artistic residence. Since moving there the sea has continued to imprint itself on her mindscreen and she brings these often intense images to life through various techniques.

Her work conveys the deep sense of respect and passion she feels for the ocean through a clean and intense style. Daniela's artwork has been featured in several galleries across Europe and her art has been auctioned at Christies's NY Green Auction.

Daniela Garreton (1983) es una artista del País Vasco. Nació en Santiago de Chile. Creciendo en un país devastador con más de 4.000 km de costa variada, el mar pronto se convirtió en la pasión de su vida.*

En 2010 Daniela se trasladó a Europa y eligió otra ciudad costera, San Sebastián, como su residencia artística. Desde que se movió allí el mar ha seguido imprimiéndose en su pantalla mental y ella trae estas imágenes a menudo intensas a la vida a través de diferentes técnicas.

Su trabajo transmite el profundo sentido de respeto y pasión que siente por el océano a través de un estilo limpio e intenso. Las ilustraciones de Daniela se han ofrecido en varias galerías a través de Europa y su arte se ha subastado en Christies's NY Green Auction.

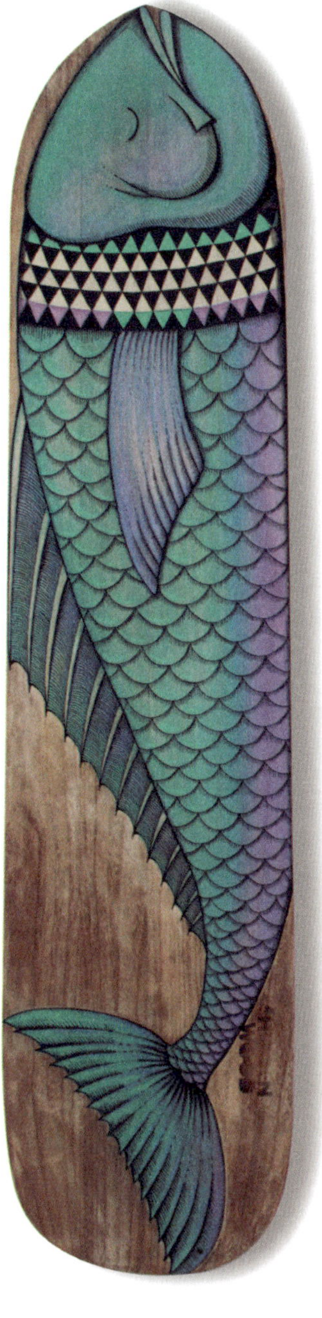

Pez alaia // by Daniela Garreton

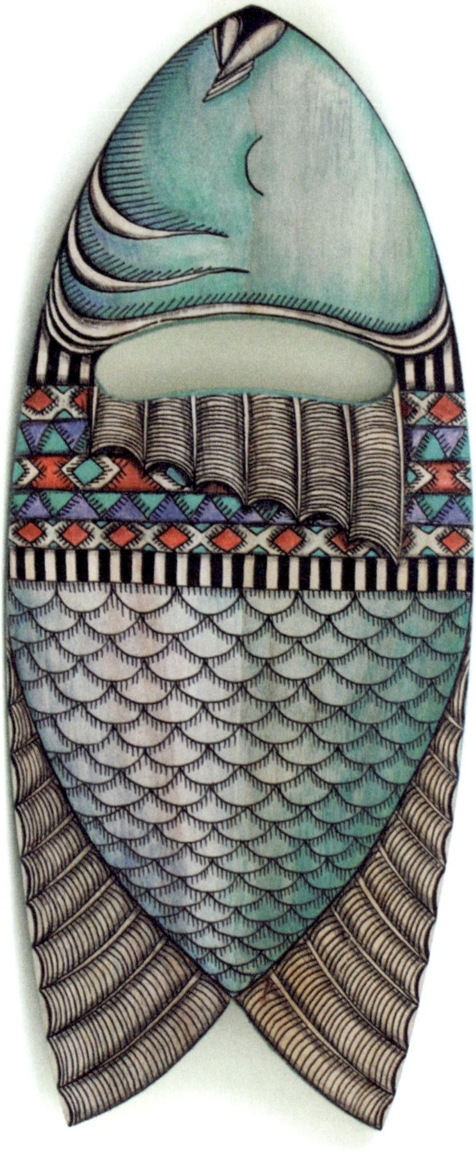

176

Handplane Parroquet fish // by Daniela Garreton

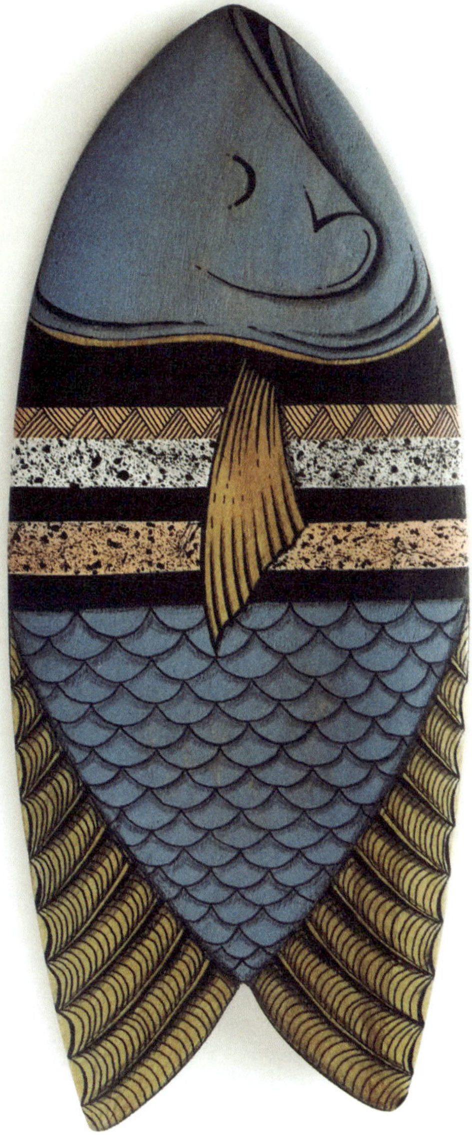

Handplane Lubina // by Daniela Garreton

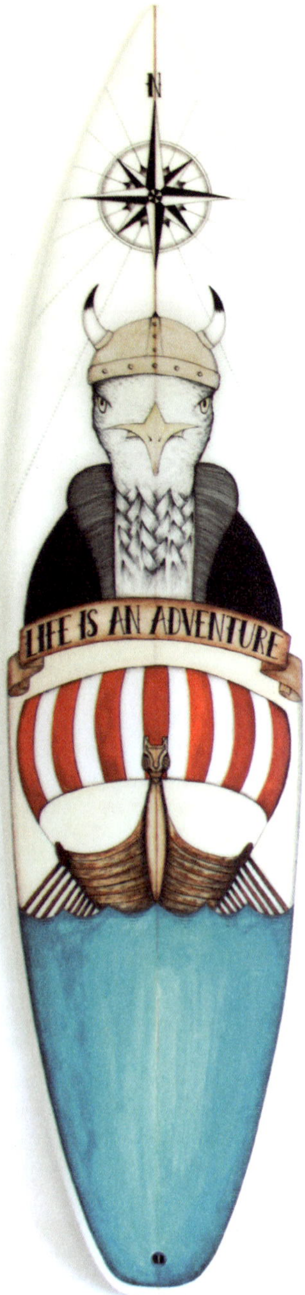

Viking seagull // by Daniela Garreton

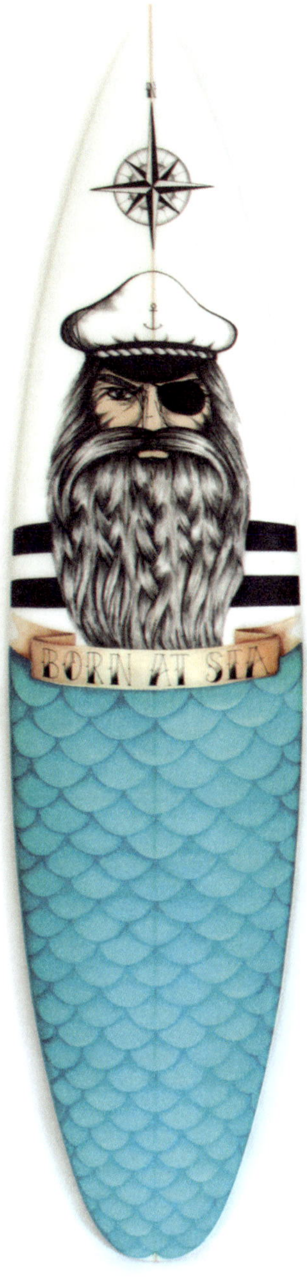

Capitan surfboard // by Daniela Garreton

Chrissy Lau

ChrissyLau.com	instagram: @deciphertheday

Chrissy Lau is an illustrator from England and now lives in Sydney, Australia. She graduated from university with a law degree but her real passion is all things creative. Her illustrations are inspired by her Chinese heritage and are instantly recognisable by her signature delicate lines, masses of flowing hair and intricate patterns. She has been a commercial illustrator for over 14 years creating designs for a vast array of clients including Samsung, Marie Claire, Sydney Opera House, Penguin, Mambo, Royal Australian Mint and Guernsey Post. Chrissy is taking on the world, one drawing at a time!

Chrissy Lau es una ilustradora de Inglaterra y ahora vive en Sydney, Australia. Se graduó en la universidad como abogada pero su pasión verdadera son todas las cosas creativas. Sus ilustraciones se inspiran en su herencia china y son instantáneamente reconocibles por su firma, líneas delicadas, masas de pelo fluido y patrones intrincados. Ha sido ilustradora comercial durante más de 14 años creando diseños para una amplia gama de clientes, incluyendo Samsung, Marie Claire, Sydney Opera House, Penguin, Mambo, Royal Australian Mint y Guernsey Post. Chrissy está recorriendo el mundo dibujo a dibujo!

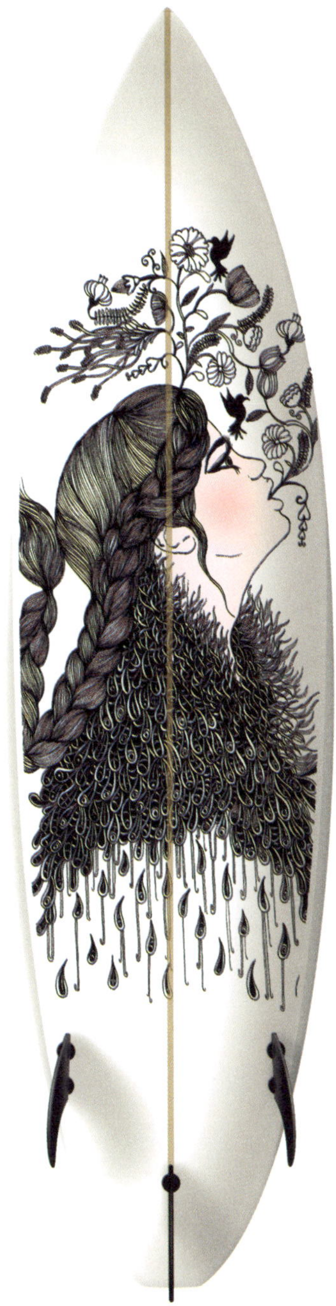

Untitled // by Chrissy Lau

Boom-art

www.boom-art.com

Known for its rare skateboards, Boom-Art, has joined forces with UWL Surfboard – one of the best surf factories in Europe to create a series of Collector's Surfboards.

Conocido por sus raros skates, Boom-Art, se unió a UWL Surfboard, una de las mejores fábricas de surf de Europa para crear una serie de tablas de surf de coleccionista.

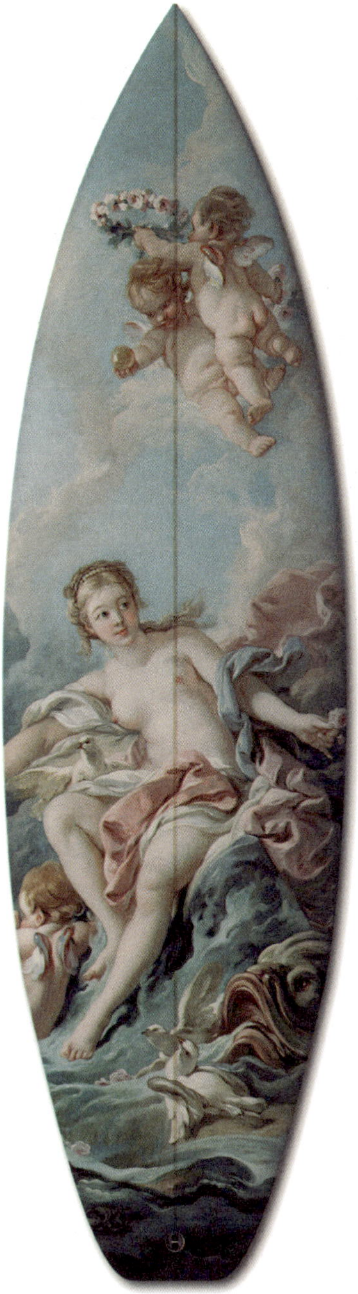

Venus // by Boom-art

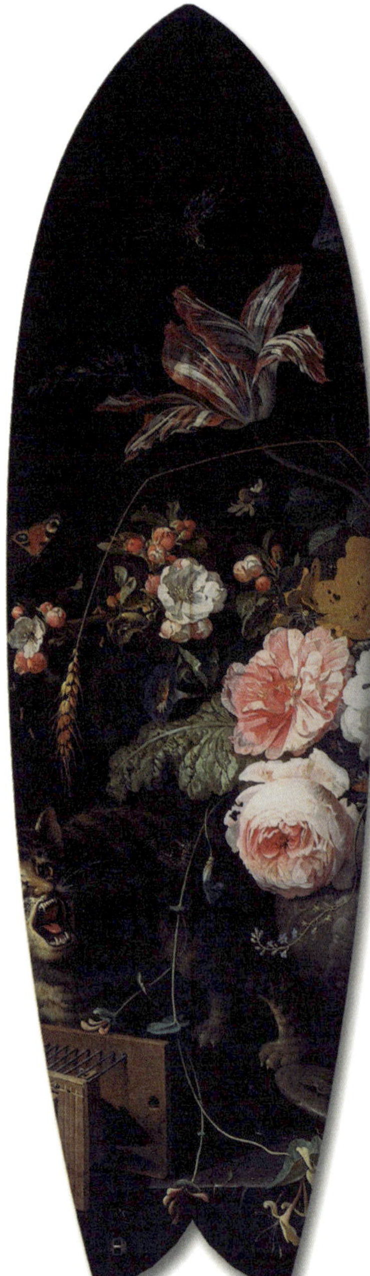

Highsnobiety // by Boom-art

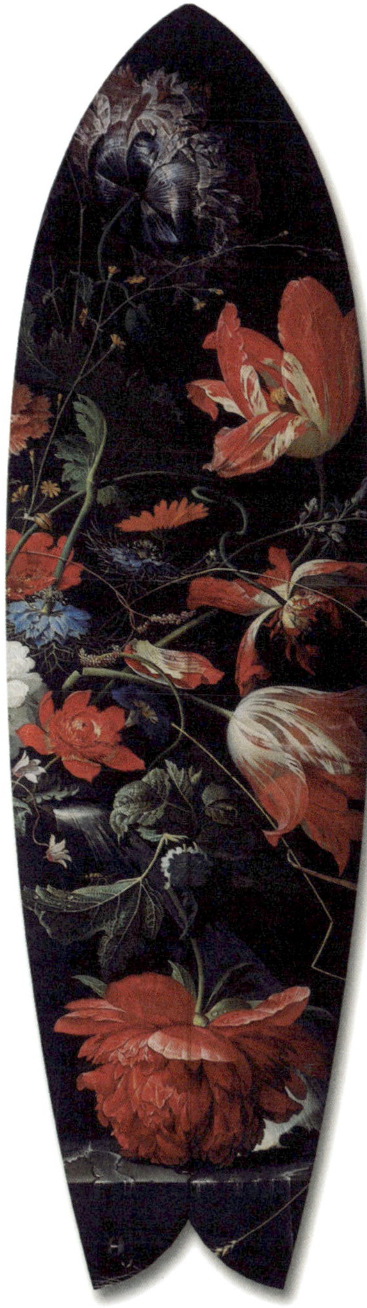

Highsnobiety // by Boom-art

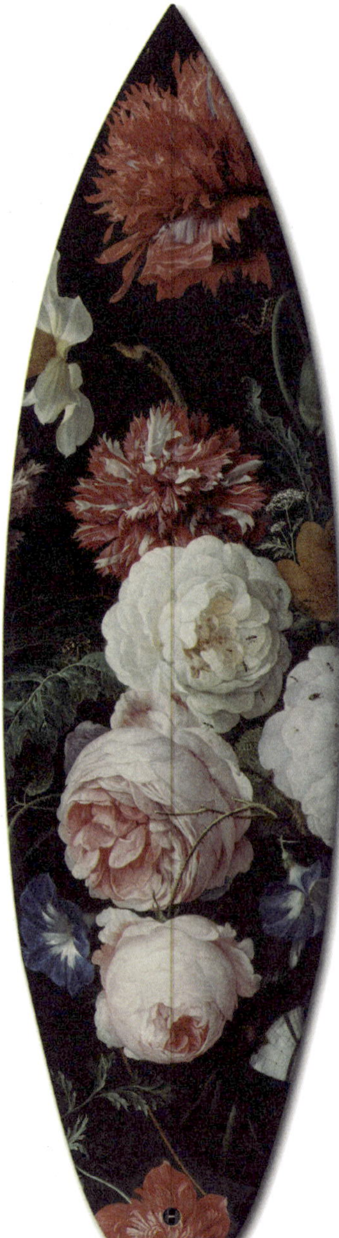

Flowers // by Boom-art

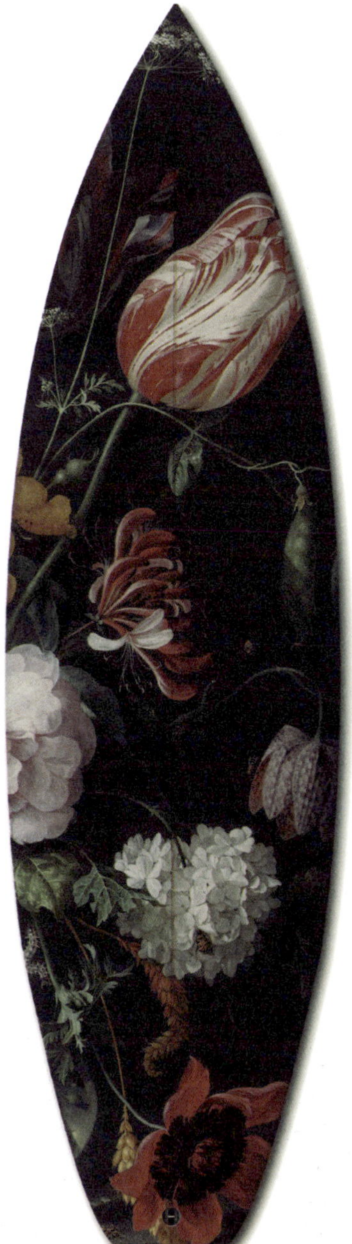

Flowers // by Boom-art

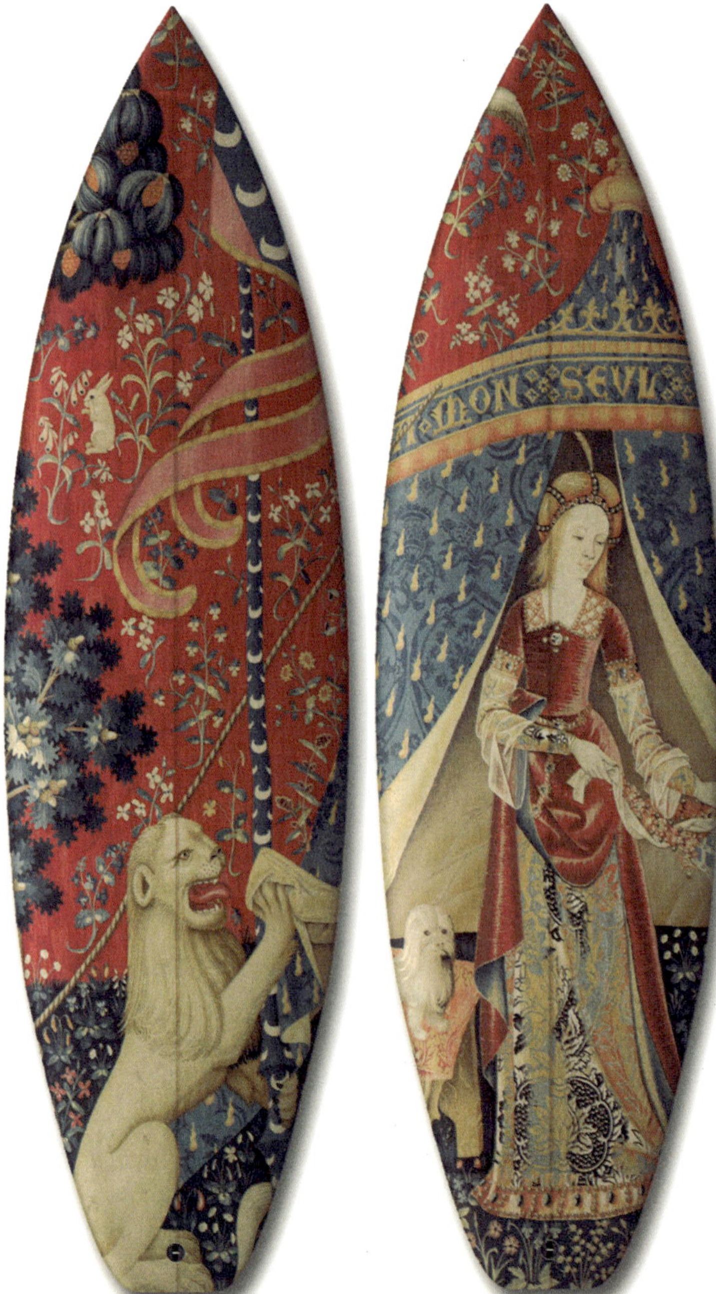

Lady and the Unicorn // by Boom-art

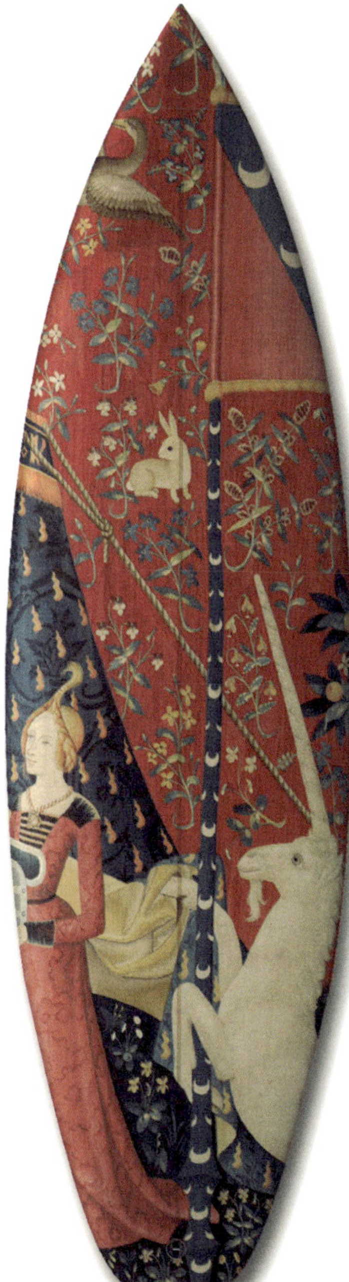

Lady and the Unicorn // by Boom-art